# 3 A.M. Stories

by
Mark Maier

**DSM**
STORYFORGE

Published by DSM Story Forge

Copyright © 2022 DSM Story Forge

All rights reserved. No part of this publication may be reproduced, distributed, or transmitted in any form or by any means, including photocopying, recording, or other electronic or mechanical methods, without the prior written permission of the publisher, except in the case of brief quotations embodied in critical reviews and certain other noncommercial uses permitted by copyright law. For permission requests, write to the publisher, addressed "Attention: Permissions Coordinator," at the address below.

ISBN: 979-8-9861562-1-7 (Paperback)
ISBN: 979-8-9861562-6-2 (eBook)

Any references to historical events, real people, or real places are used fictitiously. Names, characters, and places are products of the author's imagination.

Book design by Joe Deptowicz
(joe@winmorecolumbus.com)

Published by DSM Story Forge, LLC in the United States of America.

First printing edition 2022.

DSM Story Forge
1733 Boulder Court
Powell, OH 43065

www.dsmstoryforge.com

Dedicated to Carrie and Niall, Allen and Brittany,
And the next generation

CONTENTS

Prestigious Perspective

S.O.S.

Defined

Pocket Watch

Blossom

Front Row

Seen One, Take One

Without Rain

Identity

Umm...

Breathe

Holy Place

Moment

Exercising

Listen Here

Safe Place

Awaken

Peace

Exposed

Beauty

'Til Death

Do Our Part

Renew Within

In The Dark

Gathering Place

Along The Water's Edge

Accountability

Taken Aback

Dreaming

Quirkiness

Finders Keepers

From The Vista

Mirage

Not Resigning

When Enough Is Too Much

Dry Spell

Like Thoughts Crowding My Mind

Inevitable

Nobody Knows

Life

For The Record

Subsist

Escape

Presence

Protection

Wedding Announcement

Sling & A Stone

Jeremy

Bitter

Room Without A View

Driven

Friday Night Into Saturday Morning

Ghost Town

Certain Age

Word Breath

Cleansing

No Doubt

Eventual

3 A.M.

Equation

Prestigious Perspective

When I began to speak up,
I found I am speaking out.

When I began to speak out
I found I am questioning the world.

When I began to question the world,
I found the world did not answer.

When the world did not answer,
I began to doubt myself.

When I began to die inside,
I found more of a desire to live.

S.O.S.

I wish I could
Do this
On my own,
But I can't –
An affable smile
Isn't worth
The energy.

So, I whisper
God's name
Into the dark

And while
Waiting
For the morning
Rush hour
God
      Whispers
           Back

Pocket Watch

Pull out the time –
Still there.
I put it back
Where it belongs
Until I check it again
Later
To see if it's still
Breathing.

Blossom

How do I become
A psalm
On the heart
Of God.

Wait on
Him
To do
The writing,
Allowing
Him
To control
The pen,
For it is
Him
Who masters
The exact
Ebb and flow
Of life's
Current

Front Row

The little boy
A couple tables over
Chugs his drink —
Juice? Water?
Something else?
I can't tell
Because he slurps
It up and begins
Sucking air
Before his thirst
Seems quenched.

His father
Is distracted
By a phone call.
His mother
Is distracted
By his brother,
Younger and tiny —
The age
Of incompetency,
Though not completely,
But learning
To grow up.

Is this family
As empty
As the little boy's
Plastic cup?

How quickly
Does the spirit
Get sucked
Through the straw
Until there
Is nothing
But the sound
Of gurgling air
Coming through
The relationships?

I've heard
There are
Free refills.

Seen One, Take One

A moment
A lifetime
A handout

A truth
A world
A heart

A love
A peace
A fluke

Stroke
      of
           luck

Something
         of
             worth

Brand
      new
          day

A question
A way
A hopefulness

Doors
    opened
        wide

A road
A picture
A memory

Paths
    traveled
        together

Without Rain

The skies did not
Open wide enough
For the rains
To fall.
The clouds would not
Shed a single tear.

The gusts of wind
Sent blazing fires
And downing trees
And tumbling shingles
Everywhere around.

But the rains
Refused to come
To cleanse
The area
Of this windy
Pandemonium.

Identity

Who am I?
Who am I
    To fully
    Understand
Who I am?

Umm...

Being held hostage
Until just the right moment
In time.

This musical rest
This unavoidable silence.
This relentless quiet.

Only ruined by noise,
A muffled contrast
Of what should have been.

Sucking the void
Out of a much needed
Pause

      That will never
Be returned, tangled
In whims of clatter.

Oh, no matter,
No accident,
No understanding.

No time to process,
To hoist up knowledge
And think, now.

Waiting patiently
For postmortem,
Awarded post-humorously.

Breathe

*To be a Christian without prayer is no more possible than to be alive without breathing.*
*– Martin Luther*

Exhale –
There is a need
For submission.

In order
To reach
Freedom.

There's so much
To do –
There's too much!

Step back
And want...
No need
To rush.
Giving a sigh
Of relief.

Inhale –
Close the door
For the privacy.

There is not
A punishment
For the blemishes.

Come into
The presence
Of God
With a name
That is feared
And is filling.

And the rewards
Will increase
As the hunger
Is eased.

Holy Place

To be anywhere
With an awareness
Of God's presence
Is appointment
Within a sanctuary
In that dwelling.

Moment

A man glances
A baby cries
A siren screams
A dog barks
A cat purrs
A woman reveals
A child giggles
A day turns
A night blossoms
A light fades

And blessings happen

Exercising

Walking with God
Is good
      For the heart
And keeps faith
Running
      Through
            The veins

Listen Here

My pride should send me
To an early grave.
My soul is a city
Besieged by evil –
I am shameful for this.

I've cried out in prayer,
Wondering
If my broken spirit
Reaches a listening ear.

But to find peace
I need a quieter soul.
Or maybe I need peace
To silence this soul
Altogether.

How? I cry out again…

This could be considered
Karma because I should get
What I deserve –

However, this time I find
A piece of the Almighty
Within all this debris.

Safe Place

We are a meticulously odd bunch
Living in our own pre-historic times –
Telling stories of our own pasts
With other connoisseurs of coffee, lattes
And various alcoholic beverages.

Conversations arise and then pass
Without a fleeting thought
Of what was truly meant to be.
We are full of emptiness
But yearn for acknowledgement.

One man speaks up, alleging aloud
He is a good person. Everyone nearby
Looks up stunned and, as if
In unison, says "aren't we all?"
Before eyes averting away.

Awaken

In the morning
There is silence
In the dwelling.

In the morning
The only noise
Is just outside.

In the morning
I am hungry
For much more.

In the morning
Someone else perished
In their slumber.

In the morning
I am here
Hiding in peace.

In the morning
The mist hangs
Low, above ground.

In the morning,
Chasing the dawn
In all confidence.

In the morning
I'm quickly thankful
For waking today.

Peace

Carnations on a windowsill
Dripping with beauty
Supported by sunlight

No agony or grief
Or any disbelief

Just the acceptance
Of God's
      Divine company

Exposed

Running naked
Through
The sands
Of time –
This is inevitable
Because
God sees
Everything
Anyways.

Beauty

I poked the eye
Of the Beholder
Just to draw
Some attention.

That didn't work well.

I attempted punching
The eye
Of the Beholder.

That did not work either.

Instead, I stop pestering
The Beholder.
My attention
Is given
Elsewhere.

My children arrived,
Each receiving
A welcoming hug.

And I noticed
The Beholder
Gawking.

'Til Death

The seven days of mourning
Have lasted seven years
And going on seven more.

When will the eighth day
Come? Bringing freedom!
Bringing resemblance of relief!

There is a lack of breathable air –
I am short of breath – rapid, fleeting –
Inside this coffin of time.

Just need to take breaths – slow, steady.
Concentrate. Concentrate. Concentrate.
It's so difficult to concentrate.

This must be a kind of trap.
There are loud banging noises
Like someone hammering nails.

The pounding is not uncommon.
But comes at irregular intermissions.
Sometime louder. Sometimes softer.

Someone is sending me early
To a grave, but aren't' I
Already at that point?

The whispering in the pews
Becomes jumbled – grasping –
Carrying empty conversations.

Do Our Part

I dreamed of familiar faces,
Dressed in black and sadness,
Sitting beside the one honored.
I speak much appreciation
As to their presence here – life.

There is a section of that lifespan
Crumbled, crumpled together –
Years fallen into abyss.
Wasted away by anger, misery.
Wishing to take that time back.

A spiritual quarrel screams
Incoherently inside the mind,
Causing extreme thirst in the soul,
But the life inside passes away
Alone behind fastened doors.

The reign came for cleansing
That changes the worlds –
Personally, and globally –
The price allows for unrestricted
Shipping and handling.

Heads bent forward in prayer,
Eyes closed, and hands folded,
Not knowing what we've done
Or what we're doing –
We just do what we do.

Without accepting just cause
For our actions. Or accept
The justification of a source
Abundantly higher than our own.
Healing our soul from impaired vision.

Renew Within

The dog lays
On one end
Of the couch.
The cat steady
On the windowsill
Looking at night.
My wife asleep
In another room.

All of us waiting
For morning to rise –

For the sun to shine
On our differences
And our similarities.

Will we come out
Of the dark stages
In shackles or
Rubbing our wrists
From our recent
Release into freedom?

Will we be dancing
On air or will we
Remain weighted down?

Come back!
Rise up!

Shed new light
On our spirits
So we may
Enjoy the day
With new eyes.

In The Dark

The neighbors talk
At the table
On their patio.

They work their
Business
While I mind
Mine.

The crickets drown
The (not so) neighborly
Conversation,
Not that I worry about
What they're saying
Anyways.

I head inside,
Leaving them
In summer's night.

Gathering Place

In a few hours
They'll collect
In groups
Over coffee
Or breakfast
Or anywhere else
They can conference
Face-to-face,
Making confessions
About last night.

Old men will
Dream dreams
And the young
Will be prayed
Upon.

Calm will hang
In limbo
Over everyone's
Irreconcilable
Differences.
Some of them
Shouldn't breath
In the same stale room
With one another.

Along The Water's Edge

At this place
People fell in love,
While love
Falls into people.

Spiritual makeovers
Materialize here.

Taking on the challenges
When the storms
Roll through.

Taking on the peace
When the sun
Rises afresh.

I once dreamt big
Along these shores,
Throwing aspirations
To the horizons
Only to find out
How they would
Sink after so many
Jumps on top
Of the water.

Then dragging the wait
A little longer (for effect)
To find out if there
Is any worth
In having patience.

Maybe I was finding
Aspirations
Along the wrong
Shoreline.

No worries.
This too
Shall pass
Into the good
Night.

Accountability

We are here
Because all parts
Are created equal.

We are here
Because of the
Oath we share.

We are here
Because we see
Truth, justice, life.

We are here
Because we are
Established under God.

We are here
Because you are
In each person.

We are here
Because the change
Has come again.

We are here
Because we have
To stand firm –

To stand tall –
To stand proud –
To stand open.

The road ahead
Is lined with
Challenges – good, bad.

We are unable
To do this
All by ourselves.

Let us accept
The fresh air –
Inhaling – breathe deep.

Let us accept
A corner turned,
What lay ahead.

Hold my hand,
I hold yours –
Never the same.

Are you serious?

Empowered by people

For the people!

Taken Aback

In the midst
Of the mess,
I do not realize
Where I am
Until too late.
The damage done
Because the midwife
Ready to help
Birth
    Bitterness
    Anger
    Depression
All leaches
To the soul
Already weakened
And ready to walk away.

The mess
Wreaks havoc
Little by little
On the conscious
Then the subconscious.

Nothing is in place
To dissuade

The determination
Of the termites
Hunger
To bring down
The house.

The brutality
Originally
Came through words –
The mess was
Vocally meant
To destroy.

Now, silence
That is supposedly
A golden opportunity
Grows, gnaws
Generously
In an effort
To devastate
Whatever moral,
Or mortal,
Foundation
That is left.

And I lay
Shattered
And distraught

In the darkness
Sensing coldness,
Sensing walls
　　　closing inward.

And the dog
Deeply sighs,
Bringing back
A sense
Of reality
In this moment.

So I move –
Stand up
And walk.
The walls
Reach out
And hold me
Steady,
Vertical.

Dreaming

Stress free sleep
Stops by sometimes –

Tonight's
 The night –

Finally!

Quirkiness

Everybody has their
Mannerisms –
You have yours,
I have mine.

And we'll change
For nobody else
Except ourselves.

Do those quirks
Make us selfish?
Or allow us
To stand out
As individuals?

Finders Keepers

We just arrived home –
The neighborhood is quiet –
The house is quiet –
And the pets are sleeping,
And quiet.

This could be
Misconstrued
As unusual
For a summer's night
In this neighborhood.

We are grateful
For nights like this,
For every night
Like this
Separates us
From the drama
Of when we returned
To find this house,
Our home,
Was invaded
By thieves.

I sometimes
Find myself

Praying for those
Crooks – those
Who are too scared
To take on
The responsibilities
Of their actions.

Now is a time
For a deep breath,
The original calmness
Of arriving home
Has now become refocused
On anger and fear
Of that dark time –
For another year
Has passed.

This is beyond time
To forgive and forget
But I still hold
Onto something
So deep inside
That I can't seem
To overlook.

The grudges should
Not have come –
I need to forgive

One more time
>	For the line crossed
>	For the security (and privacy) invaded
>	For the people who have done wrong

Peace be with you.

From The Vista

The 24-hour restaurant,
At this house,
Houses the bar flies
Trying to sober up
Before heading home
To spouses –
To children –
To parents –
To roommates –
To nobody.

The crowd throbs
Then slowly flows
As 2-by-2
With friends,
As strangers
They leave the curb
Only to return
This time tomorrow.

Sirens crescendo somewhere
In the distance –
Someone's tried
To make the trek
Home without a glitch –
Someone didn't get there

Mirage

The apartments are great
Tonight
    Unusually quiet.

The police helicopter,
A normal fixture
In the night sky,
Must be hovering
Elsewhere in the city
Or parked for the evening.

There still might be
Something illegal
Taking place
Behind closed doors.

Nobody even drives
Through the parking lot —
Usually busy now.
Nobody even drives
Up and down the streets
With their music's volume
Turned up.

Where is everybody presently?
Is this their night off?

This may be
Cause for concern –
This is out of the ordinary.

Should there be reason
For fear to rise?
Someone may point out
This the calm
Before the storm –
We may know more
Sooner or later.

The darkness
Sounds the loudest.
The black bleakness
Offers an odd
Comfortable silence,
Camouflaging the truth.
This is a perplexing
Mind game.

Who, or what, will rise
To disrupt this tranquility?
The breeze even refuses
To make an appearance.

Not Resigning

Poised unexpectedly
Along the roadside,
Another of life's
Slowdowns.
Everyone else
Drives on –
Moving forward
Without stopping.
Doing well
For themselves
No matter the time.

Stranded unexpectedly
Alone and wondering
What will happen
In the end.

Not driven
Like everyone else
Down the same roads,
And getting off
At the same exits –
Life flying past
Surprisingly self-confident.
In the wrong direction.

# Dedication

Dedicated to John Maynard, John Trundle, and other "Johns" who did not necessarily bear the name of John but filled his role of introducing me to Jesus, the Lamb of God.

And

For Dr. Frederick Kellogg, who patiently taught me to love New Testament Greek and *John's* wonderful story of Jesus.

> *"The core of the gospel is not just being addressed and being claimed; it is telling a story. If the messianic age begins with the announcement of the good news, then everyone must join in telling the story of this new future."*
>
> *"The Four Gospels tell the story of Jesus as history of his messianic mission. The Acts of the Apostles tell the story of the church of Jesus as an eschatological exodus story. The Christian community is a story-telling community; it tells the story of Jesus with bread and wine as the story of its hope "until he comes." It tells its own history of communion with Jesus—its history of suffering and its hope for history—and this is the way the church proclaims the gospel."*
>
> **Jurgen Moltman**

A
# STORYTELLER
LOOKS AT

# The Gospel of John

Charles W. Maynard

Market Square
BOOKS

A Storyteller Looks at
*The Gospel of John*
by Charles Maynard

©2022 Charles Maynard

books@marketsquarebooks.com
141 N. Martinwood Dr., Knoxville TN 37923

ISBN: 978-1-950899-69-2

Printed and Bound in the United States of America
Cover Illustration & Book Design ©2022 Market Square Publishing, LLC

Editor: Sheri Carder Hood
Page Designer: Carrie L. Rood
Cover Artist: Kevin Slimp
Post-Production Editor: Ken Rochelle

All rights reserved. No part of this book may be reproduced in any manner without written permission except in the case of brief quotations included in critical articles and reviews. For information, please contact Market Square Publishing, LLC.

**Scripture quotations used with permission from:**

### CEB
Scripture quotations from the COMMON ENGLISH BIBLE. © Copyright 2011 COMMON ENGLISH BIBLE. All rights reserved. Used by permission. (www.CommonEnglishBible.com).

### ESV
The Holy Bible: English Standard Version
Scripture quotations marked "ESV" are taken from The Holy Bible: English Standard Version, copyright © 2001, Wheaton: Good News Publishers. Used by permission. All rights reserved.

### MSG
Scripture quotations marked MSG are taken from THE MESSAGE, copyright © 1993, 2002, 2018 by Eugene H. Peterson. Used by permission of NavPress, represented by Tyndale House Publishers. All rights reserved.

### NRSV
New Revised Standard Version Bible, copyright © 1989 National Council of the Churches of Christ in the United States of America. Used by permission. All rights reserved worldwide.

### NIV
Scriptures marked NIV are taken from the NEW INTERNATIONAL VERSION (NIV): Scripture taken from THE HOLY BIBLE, NEW INTERNATIONAL VERSION ®. Copyright© 1973, 1978, 1984, 2011 by Biblica, Inc.™. Used by permission of Zondervan.

### J.B. Phillips
Scripture quotations marked "Phillips" are taken from The New Testament in Modern English, copyright © 1958, 1959, 1960 J.B. Phillips and 1947, 1952, 1955, 1957 The Macmillian Company, New York. Used by permission. All rights reserved.

# Table of Contents

Introduction: About Four O'clock in the Afternoon . . . . . . . 1

Chapter One: How to Read . . . . . . . . . . . . . . . . . . . . . . . . . 9

Chapter Two: John the Storyteller . . . . . . . . . . . . . . . . . . . 31

Chapter Three: Weaving the Tapestry . . . . . . . . . . . . . . . . 45

Chapter Four: I Am . . . . . . . . . . . . . . . . . . . . . . . . . . . . . . 67

Chapter Five: Signs of the Times . . . . . . . . . . . . . . . . . . . 83

Chapter Six: Pitching the Tent, Glory Be! . . . . . . . . . . . . 107

Epilogue: . . . . . . . . . . . . . . . . . . . . . . . . . . . . . . . . . . . . 121

Meditations on the Gospel of John . . . . . . . . . . . . . . . . . . 123

    Words and the Word . . . . . . . . . . . . . . . . . . . . . . . . . 125

    What Is So Little Among So Many? . . . . . . . . . . . . . . . 135

    A Blind Man . . . . . . . . . . . . . . . . . . . . . . . . . . . . . . . 141

    The Heart and Mind of Christ . . . . . . . . . . . . . . . . . . . 151

    The Comforter . . . . . . . . . . . . . . . . . . . . . . . . . . . . . 161

    Fanning the Flames . . . . . . . . . . . . . . . . . . . . . . . . . 175

    Breakfast on the Beach . . . . . . . . . . . . . . . . . . . . . . . 183

Resources: . . . . . . . . . . . . . . . . . . . . . . . . . . . . . . . . . . . 191

# Introduction
# About Four O'clock in the Afternoon

Ask anyone to list three of their favorite verses in the entire Bible, and one of the three will be probably from the *Gospel of John*. "For God so loved the world..." (3:16); "Let not your heart be troubled..." (14:1); "I won't leave you an orphan..." (14:18); "Jesus wept." (11:35, famously the shortest verse in scriptures); to name only a few.

Ask the same people to name three of their favorite books in the Bible, and often the list will include the *Gospel of John. John* is very accessible to people. It has been favored down through the ages. The other three gospels have been regarded as wonderful to study, but *John* is seen as the one to read.

I recently noticed a Facebook post in which a person wrote: "If you don't know Jesus, please read the *Gospel of John* in the New Testament. You will find yourself awed by this Savior who loved you enough to die for you."

A tapestry is a cloth fabrication made of horizontal threads called "weft" woven through vertical threads called "warps." The weft is tamped down so closely that the warps cannot be seen. The design or picture of a tapestry is in the weft, and the attention to detail is incredible. The weft is knotted and spliced to have different colors and textures form a picture or design.

Tapestries have hung in dwellings for centuries. Sometimes they carried scenes from stories that were important to families and communities. Thick tapestries were often hung on the walls of drafty rooms to keep the space warm on cold winter nights.

In my life, quilts have been more familiar and common than tapestries. Patchwork quilts are made from cloth scraps. Ingenious and thrifty seamstresses took bits of old shirts, dresses, coats, tablecloths, sheets, or blankets and pieced them together into squares. The squares were then arranged into traditional patterns: Wedding Ring, Double Wedding Ring, Tulip, Railroad, Log Cabin, Pinwheel, Rose of Sharon, God's Eye, Friendship, to name only a few.

Quilt squares are joined together to form a top. Batting is then put between the top and a backing cloth. The "quilting" is the needlework that binds the three layers together, and it is judged based on its uniformity and design. The lines of thread sometimes highlight the pattern of the squares. Other times, it adds themes not present in the squares.

On a chair in my study, I have a small quilt that women of a church I served made for me. They knew of my love for the mountains and waterfalls, so they stitched mountain peaks and swirling waters into the quilt. It is beautiful, but if you don't look at all of it, you will miss the story and the artistry.

My dad loved piecing jigsaw puzzles. He liked puzzles with at least one-thousand pieces. Sometimes our dining room table was covered with three-thousand and five-thousand pieces! He patiently bent over the table constructing wonderful pictures. Copacabana Beach in Rio, sailboats on Lake Geneva, Golden Aspen in the Rockies, snow-covered peaks in the Alps, the Grand Canyon.

Dad, however, did not enjoy taking the puzzles apart and re-boxing them. He decided to keep the pictures by sliding them onto a thin sheet of Masonite, gluing them down, and then attaching them to the wall of our den. After years, the den walls were completely covered in picture puzzles.

The intent of this book is to look at the tapestry, so to speak, of *John's* gospel. The needlework, the knots, and the splices (which form the marvelous picture) grant the reader an appreciation for the artistry and style of the author. Observing a quilt being made at a "quilting" does not negate the beauty and warmth of the quilt, but it does make one grateful for the work that went into creating it. A stack of boxes filled with puzzles is not as fascinating as a room of completed puzzles with all their colorful scenes.

Ray Hicks, the quintessential mountain storyteller (recognized as a National Heritage Fellow by the National Endowment for the Arts) captured my attention the first time I heard him. Ray told stories every year at the National Storytelling Festival in Jonesborough, Tennessee, from its beginning in 1973 until his death in 2003.

As Ray neared the end of his life, I joined several

other storytellers in a pilgrimage to Ray and Rosa Hick's house on Beech Mountain in the western North Carolina mountains. As we stepped on the porch, we dumped firewood we had carried from the road on to stacks near the door.

Ray was weak from his battle with cancer. He sat up and greeted us warmly. We were simply paying a call to this great storyteller. Of course, after a while, Ray began telling stories, and we egged him on.

Someone said, "Ray, tell about the time the cow ate your britches."

"Yes, yes!" we said. We had all heard the story but were eager to enjoy it again. We wanted to hear Ray's voice and accent, his unique way of presenting any adventure.

He began the familiar tale, one from his teen years. However, as he went along, he suddenly stopped and said, "You hear that part right there? That didn't happen to me. It happened to my cousin. I thought it fit into this story right well."

He continued, stopping every now and again to explain where or when that particular part had happened. I had always thought of "the britches tale" as a whole piece of cloth. Instead, what Ray showed us that afternoon was a "garment" constructed of different events. He turned the story inside out so we could see the seams where he put it together.

When he finished, amid our laughter and applause, he said, "The first time I told that story, my cousin was sitting in the audience. He come up to me afterwards and said, 'Ray! That ain't so!' I said, 'No, but there's some so in it.'"

*John* the author has stitched together a mighty telling of the story of Jesus. Interestingly, he does not include any of Jesus' parables (stories). Instead, he relates Jesus' life as the story itself.

*John* knows the strongest vessel in which to carry truth is through story. It is the way we humans remember and communicate. If you want information or truth to survive for generations, wrap it in a story.

One approach to interpreting scripture is called "narrative criticism." In this school of thought, form and literary criticism (which are also legitimate approaches in their own right) are put aside in order to consider the narrative being told. Many works and courses are taught on this way of seeing scripture.

After the poetic prologue (John 1:1-18), Jesus' story begins not with his birth or baptism, but when John the Baptizer sees Jesus and says:

> *Look! The Lamb of God who takes*
> *away the sins of the world!*
>
> **John 1:29**

The author of *John* leaves no doubt as to the purpose of the gospel book. The narrative continues:

> *I have seen and testified that this one is God's son.*
>
> **John 1:34.**

"The next day John the Baptizer told two of his students, 'Look! The Lamb of God!' Then Andrew (one of the two students) went to his brother Simon and said, 'We have found the Messiah!'" (1:41). Another person who ran into Jesus, Philip (who was from the same hometown as Andrew and Simon) told his friend, Nathaniel, "We have found the one Moses wrote about in the Law and the Prophets: Jesus, Joseph's son, from Nazareth." (1:45) After Nathanael met Jesus, he said, "Rabbi, you are God's Son. You are the king of Israel" (1:49).

Just in case the reader still does not understand, *John* quotes Jesus as saying, "You will see greater things than these! I assure you that you will see heaven open and God's angels going up to heaven and down to earth on the Human One" (1:50b-51).

A couple of things strike me about this first scene in the narrative of *John*. One is an odd little detail. The unnamed disciple, who had been following John the Baptizer, remembered his first encounter with Jesus. "It was about four o'clock in the afternoon." Very precise. Not sometime that day or even sometime that afternoon. Not two or three or five o'clock, but four o'clock p.m.! The writer never forgot the moment he met Jesus.

John Wesley journaled about his life-changing encounter with Jesus with similar specificity:

> *In the afternoon I was asked to go to St Paul's. The anthem was, "Out of the deep have I called unto thee, O Lord. Lord, hear my voice. O let thine ears consider well the voice of my complaint. If thou, Lord, wilt be extreme to mark what is done amiss, O Lord, who may abide it? But there is mercy*

*with thee; therefore thou shalt be feared....O Israel, trust in the Lord: For with the Lord there is mercy, and with him is plenteous redemption. And he shall redeem Israel from all his sins."*

*In the evening I went very unwillingly to a society in Aldersgate Street, where one was reading Luther's Preface to the Epistle to the Romans. About a quarter before nine, while he was describing the change which God works in the heart through faith in Christ, I felt my heart strangely warmed. I felt I did trust in Christ, Christ alone for salvation, and an assurance was given me that he had taken away my sins, even mine, and saved me from the law of sin and death.*

**John Wesley**
The Journal, May 24, 1738

Wesley never forgot the moment. It was 8:45 p.m. Stunning. Precise. The writer of *John* has the same memory. Other meetings with the Divine are well remembered. Samuel in the temple at night. Saul on the road to Damascus. Andrew, Peter, James, and John fishing along the beach. Interestingly, the last scene in *John* occurs in the half-light of dawn.

There is an immediacy to the telling of Jesus' story in *John*. It is important to the author that the listeners/readers see and hear Jesus, because *John* knows that is how others come to believe in Jesus. The entire book is about meeting Jesus. We should look at the *Gospel of John* as a well-told story, one so carefully and skillfully told that all might see Jesus.

**Notice – A Lot of Johns!**

Please note there are a lot of Johns in this book, as well as in the *Gospel of John*. To better keep them straight, I refer to the first John we meet in the gospel as "John the Baptizer." (John the Baptist sounds too much like a denominational label.) I refer to the *Gospel of John* in italics, sometimes shortening it to *John*. *John* the author is italicized as well to better connect him to the *Gospel of John*. The disciple John is interestingly never named in the *Gospel of John* (more on that later). Enjoy keeping them straight.

CHAPTER ONE
# How to Read...

**A Book**

Reading is one of the passions in my life. Before I could read, I loved to flip through books and magazines with pictures. We had a set of encyclopedias at home as well as other books. My grandfather collected *National Geographic* magazines and a wide range of books. I lived for trips to the public library. As I entered first grade, the school library opened even more doors.

I learned to read, much like my whole generation, with Dick, Jane, Sally, and Spot. However, once I got the hang of reading, I quickly tired of the rather boring antics of that crew and was ready for other adventures.

Stories were a big part of my upbringing. Naturally, I gravitated to books that told stories. History and biography caught my imagination. I remember a juvenile historical fiction series of biographies. While reading one about Davy Crockett, I suddenly realized I could SEE the scene. I was no longer reading the book. I was IN the book. It was great!

Donald Davis's *Writing as a Second Language* offers wonderful insights. His premise suggests that the first language we learn is oral, not written.[1]

It is a language of sound which carries meaning and intent, sometimes not even in words. Robert Frost had a theory of poetry he called "the sound of sense." Both Davis, a storyteller, and Frost, a poet, used written language to convey meaning. However, both are adept at communicating with the sense of the spoken word through the written word.

Some call our present times "post-literate." People can read. They just don't. You would think that everyone who can read would know how to read a book. Surprisingly, I have found this is not necessarily true. Here are a few tips on reading that may sound basic but aren't always embraced.

**First and foremost:**

1. **Read the WHOLE Book.** This is easier if you've chosen a book that interests you. Read the WHOLE book, including the introduction and epilogue. Sometimes those two pieces frame the picture.

   I don't read books a few sentences at a time. Nor do I read a few sentences on pages 15 and 16 and then a few sentences from pages 38 and 39. I don't read one paragraph one day and then another paragraph the next. I try to make time to read for at least half an hour. I read through in the order in which the author wrote.

---

[1] Donald Davis, *Writing as A Second Language,* August House, 2005.

2. **Choose a Topic or Type of Literature that Interests You.** Reading through an entire library would be a rather unusual goal. My wife tried as a kid. She didn't make it through the A section of fiction. If you like history, go for it! You may be into science fiction. All the better! Perhaps you like a good romance. You are more likely to read a whole book if you are interested in the topic, the writer, or the subject.

3. **Listen to the Writer.** In my first Old Testament class in college (which also happened to be my first semester as a freshman), the professor gave a reading assignment to complete before the first class. When we arrived, we were told to get out a piece of paper for a quiz on our reading. The first and only question on the pop quiz was, "Who wrote your textbook?"

I was stunned. I had no idea. My first thought was "Who cares? It's a textbook!" When I looked around the room, I realized no one else knew the answer. We had all read the first few chapters as assigned, but no one had bothered to read the title page or the introduction.

It is important to know who wrote the book you are reading. What is their background? Have they written anything else? As you read an author, you begin to get a sense of their style.

Learn to listen to the tone or slant of an author. We often rush past how the writer is saying it in order to get to what the writer is saying. We want to know what is meant. Rarely do we pause to enjoy how a writer delivers the meaning or story.

4. **Pay Attention to the Type of Literature.** You don't read an email from a friend the same way you read a news post. You read poetry differently than you read history. Legal writing can be boring unless you are trying to win a case and are looking for precedents. Essays are read differently than novels. The type of literature determines how it is read.

   Wendell Berry is one of my favorite authors. I like everything he has written. That being said, I read his essays in one manner, his novels in another, and his poetry in yet a third way. Shakespeare wrote poetry and plays and then wrote plays in verse. You approach an astronomy textbook differently than Walt Whitman's *When I Heard The Learn'd Astronomer*. Even love letters and complaint letters are different, although they are both letters. Libraries are divided and cataloged according to literature type. You can go to the shelves and find types of books you enjoy.

5. **The End of the Book Is Important.** The plot usually has a crisis or climax near the end of a work. Do you really want to read a mystery and quit 30 pages from the end? Of course not! You have to find out if the butler really did it!

   Did the couple get together in the end? The final act of Romeo and Juliet is rather important to the play. Did right prevail? Did evil win out? What happened to the main character? Did she succeed? Did she fail? It is all at the end of the book.

My wife jokes with me about my enjoyment of biographies. She says that biographies all have the same plot, and they all end the same. Someone is born, they grow up and do things, and then they die. The same plot. But I must admit, I read them to the last breath.

John Adams' life ends after he whispers, "Jefferson lives." Jefferson's final moments ended only hours before Adams' with Jefferson wondering, "Is it the Fourth yet?" Read to the end.

## The Bible

The English word "Bible" comes from the Greek word *biblios* which means library. (We get the words bibliography and bibliophile from this root word.) The Bible is a library of sixty-six books. It is an incredible collection compiled by the church from centuries of writings. Like any library, it is filled with all types of literature.

The Bible encompasses History, Law, Poetry, Wisdom Literature, Biography, Letters (in the New Testament – LOTS of letters – some to individuals, some to churches, some to regions, some to the Church – lots of letters), Prophecy, Romance, Tragedy, Comedy, even Fiction! (Jesus' parables for instance). That being said, the suggestions for reading a book (see above) apply to reading books in the library called The Bible.

Sometimes we forget that the early church had no Bible other than Hebrew scriptures and oral tradition (stories). The church came first—THEN the scriptures. The early church shaped the scriptures while at the same time being shaped by the tradition. Is the Bible the Word of God? Does the Bible contain the Word of God? Or does the Bible point to the Word of God?

In my own faith tradition, we believe the Bible REVEALS the Word of God. The library of faith (the Bible) sharpens our view of the Word of God, who is Jesus. As the Church developed the canon—the list of what is considered scripture, the standard was, "Did this writing reveal Jesus? Is this writing consistent with what we know and understand about the Living Word of God in Jesus Christ?"

> *The Holy Bible – We believe the Holy Bible, Old and New Testaments, reveals the Word of God so far as it is necessary for our salvation. It is to be received through the Holy Spirit as the true rule and guide for faith and practice. Whatever is not revealed in or established by the Holy Scriptures is not to be made an article of faith nor is it to be taught as essential to salvation.*
>
> **The United Methodist Church Book of Discipline 2016**
> Articles of Religion and Confession of Faith

> *The Bible reveals the Word of God – "the Bible shows us God present and active in and among living, breathing human beings, the same kind and sort of men and women that we are.*
>
> **Eugene H. Peterson**[2]

---

2  Eugene H. Peterson, *A Long Obedience in the Same Direction*, IVP, 2021, p. 199.

If we believe the Bible IS the Word of God, that would mean the early church didn't have the Word of God. The early church was born and grew with out any of what is now called the New Testament. Paul's letters and the Gospels appear later in the first century. The Church chose the writings that would be considered scripture. The Church's history and beliefs shaped the scriptures, whereupon the scriptures shaped the Church.

> *"The Bible is alive, it speaks to me; it has feet, it runs after me; it has hands, it lays hold of me."*
> **Martin Luther**

Also, if the Word of God IS the Bible, it would theoretically be possible to destroy the Word of God by getting rid of ALL the Bibles in the world. (An unlikely event, but you get the point.) Additionally, in what language is this Word of God? Is God's Word only in Greek and Hebrew or French or Latin or seventeenth century English or ...?

For centuries, most people could not read, and there were few copies of the Bible. It was read to them. People heard the scriptures. The house churches of Galatia listened to Paul's letters. The original copies of the Gospels were read aloud to gathered peoples. The idea of personal Bible reading and study is a recent development that began in the 1500s and became popular in the 1800s as more and more people could read, and Bibles were readily available.

> *This is the way the Bible has been read by most Christians for most of the Christian Centuries, but it is not commonly read that way today. The reading*

*style employed more often than not by contemporary Christians is fast, reductive, information-gathering and above all, practical. We read for what we can get out of it, what we can put to use, what we think we can use—and right now. "We...we...we...we...' all the way home."*

**Eugene Peterson**[3]

*The Bible is not primarily a source of information; it is one of the primary ways that God uses to speak to us. 'God's Word' we call it, which is to say, God's voice—God speaking to us, inviting, promising, blessing, confronting, commanding, healing.*

**Eugene Peterson**[4]

Peterson said that if we are serious about following Jesus and living life with him, we will:

*...familiarize ourselves with the world in which Jesus and his gift of life are revealed to us. We do it by reading Scriptures slowly, imaginatively, prayerfully, and obediently.*[5]

It seems that many want to imprison Jesus in the Bible. There is a movement to reverse the incarnation. To enmesh Jesus in the words of the scriptures instead of enfleshing him in daily life. "The Word became flesh, and lived among us." (John 1:14). There are those who want to confine the living, breathing, risen Jesus Christ into words, into text. The Bible uses words to show

---

3  Eugene Peterson, *A Long Obedience in the Same Direction*, IVP, 2021,p. 198.

4  Eugene Peterson, *A Long Obedience in the Same Direction*, IVP, 2021,p. 199.

5  Eugene Peterson, *A Long Obedience in the Same Direction*, IVP, 2021,p. 198.

the Word. The writer of the *Gospel of John* sought to introduce people to Jesus (John 20:30-31). For some, the advantage in confining Jesus to the Bible is so we do not have to encounter the Living Lord in day to day living. The point of the Bible is to be a window through which we can see the living Christ, Jesus, the Word of God.

> *"I take the Bible too seriously to read it literally."*
> **Karl Barth**

Biblical literalism is a recent development in the history of the Church. It became popular in the last 150 years as literacy grew and printed books became more available. The difficulty in reading the Bible literally is that it was not written that way. Additionally, literalism usually breaks down with a second language. Literalism does not work well in translation.

It is also important to remember that the divisions of chapter and verse came much later. The authors of the various books of the Biblical library did not make these divisions. Often, when I am reading a Biblical book (as opposed to studying it) I read translations or versions that do not include these divisions—*J.B. Phillips,* Eugene Peterson's *The Message,* Clarence Jordan's *Cotton Patch Version,* Reynolds Price's versions of *Mark* and *John* among others. These bring me closer to how the original books were written and heard.

Compared to the time span in which the scriptures were written, the division of the writings in chapters and verses is a recent development. In 1205, Stephen Langton, a theology professor and later Archbishop of Canterbury, divided the scriptures into chapters in order to reference sections for his commentaries on the scriptures. Cardinal Hugo of St. Cher published in 1240 a Latin Bible with the chapter divisions as they exist today. Nearly three hundred years later, a printer, Robert Estienne (or Robert Stephanus) published the New Testament (1551) and the Old Testament (1571). It is Estienne's divisions that are still used today.

Some editions of the poetry of Robert Frost and Henry Wadsworth Longfellow have line numbers as references. We rarely read the line number unless we are teaching and need to refer to it. We would not read lines 1-10, quit until the next day to read lines 11-20, and thus taking a week to read *Death of a Hired Man* or *The Psalm of Life*.

One of the difficulties in reading scripture is that unless we are reading in Greek or Hebrew, we are reading in translation. We are hearing scripture in a second language at best. Jesus came into the world to be the Word in flesh for us. As one translation puts it, "the Word became flesh and moved into the neighborhood." Jesus spoke in Aramaic, the language of his neighborhood. It is important that the Bible be read and studied in the language of the neighborhood.

It is always important to speak to people in a language they know and understand. I have had many opportunities to worship in different languages – French, Spanish, Quechua, Aymara, Haitian Creole, Arabic, Latvian, and Russian. It is a unique experience. I cannot speak or understand those languages.

Sometimes, there was an interpreter who put words into English for me. Other times I was the one speaking and worked with an interpreter. When I preached in Bolivia where there are three national languages, worship was conducted in ALL THREE languages! Thus, the sermon had to be translated into all three languages. It was tedious but fascinating as each group waited to hear the Word in their own language.

In our city, a congregation of South Sudanese refugees worships each Sunday evening. I was asked to preach to this group. When I inquired as to who would translate for me, the pastor replied, "We all work here. We all know English. We will understand you."

"Then why do you worship in Arabic?" I replied.

"Oh, Arabic is the language of our hearts. It is the language we first spoke. It is how our mothers and fathers spoke to us. We must worship God with our hearts. So we worship in Arabic."

The scriptures need to be read and heard in the language of our heart. Translating is very important. But it is difficult to translate. Robert Frost said poetry is "that which gets lost from verse and prose in translation."

The editor and poet, Stanley Burnshaw, produced *The Poem Itself,* a volume of foreign poetry (German, French, Spanish, Portuguese, and Italian). In the collection, Burnshaw "talked" the poems into English. He placed the poem in its original language at the top of the page. Next, he provided an English version of the poem, and then with footnotes talked it into English. Burnshaw's goal was to offer a "discussion aimed at enabling the reader both to understand the poem and to begin to experience. ... The aim is to help [the reader] into the poem itself." [6]

Some have resisted further translation of Biblical books, clinging to one particular version. To maintain the superiority of one translation over another is to misunderstand the nature of translation. For instance, in English we can love a pizza and love a spouse and love God. All with the same word – love. This is not possible in Greek where several words indicate various types of love. Examples of words that do not completely yield themselves to word-for-word (literal) translation are legion.

Martin Luther, in translating Latin into common German said, "We must ask the mother in the home, the children on the street, the common man in the marketplace. We must be guided by their language, by the way they speak, and do our translating accordingly."

J. B. Phillips, an English clergyman, attempted to bring the scriptures to his parishioners in a clear, current style and idiom. Phillips' own Anglican tradition relied on the authorized version (King James Version) as have many other faith traditions. "I should like to make it quite clear that I could not possibly hold the extreme "fundamentalist" position of so-called verbal inspiration. This theory is bound to break down

---

6  Stanley Burnshaw, *The Poem Itself*, Pelican Books, 1964.

sooner or later in the world of translation. There are over eleven hundred known human languages, and it was during a brief spell of work for the British and Foreign Bible Society that I learned of the attempts to translate the Bible, or at least parts of it, into nearly all of these different tongues. I learned of the extreme ingenuity which the translator must use to convey sense and truth where word-for-word transmission is out of the question."

> *You cannot talk to tribes who live without ever seeing navigable water of our possessing an anchor for the soul. You cannot speak to the Eskimos of the Lamb of God which taketh away the sin of the world, or of Christ being the true Vine and of us, his disciples, as "the branches"! Such examples could, literally, be multiplied many thousands of times. Yet I have found, when addressing meetings in this country and in America, that there still survives a minority who passionately believe in verbal inspiration. It appears that they have never seriously thought that there are millions for whom Christ died who would find a word-for-word translation of the New Testament, even if it were possible, frequently meaningless. Any man who has sense as well as faith is bound to conclude that it is the truths which are inspired and not the words which are merely the vehicles of truth."* Phillips went on to say, *"...I had never realised what a barrier beautiful but antique words had imposed.*
>
> **J. B. Phillips**
> The Ring of Truth[7]

C.S. Lewis once wrote of J.B. Phillips' translation of Colossians – "It's like seeing an old picture after it's been cleaned." This would be a good translation on the best of

---

[7] J. B. Phillips, *The Ring of Truth,* Shaw Books, 1977, page 28-29.

days. A translation that can make Jesus visible is a great translation. For the Word of God, oddly enough, is not about the words but about the Word, Jesus.

One reason I enjoy the Cotton Patch Version that Clarence Jordan produced is that he always attempted to make the meaning of the ancient original text clearer than a transliteration of word for word translation would allow.

> *There are places where it will appear that I have taken entirely too much liberty with the text. But let me point out that this is a translation of, not of Paul's words, but of his ideas. If his actual words convey the wrong impression to a modern hearer, or if they make Paul say something which he obviously did not intend, then I do scuttle his words in favor of his idea. For example, someone would be perfectly understood if he wrote to a friend, "We had hot dogs and Coke for lunch, fish and hush puppies for supper, and then sat around shooting the bull until midnight." But let that letter get lost for about two thousand years, then let some Ph.D. try to translate it into a non-English language of A.D. 3967. If he faithfully translated the words it might run something like this: "We had steaming canines (possibly a small variety such as the Chihuahua) and processed coal (the coke was probably not eaten but used to heat the dogs) for the noon meal, and fish and mute, immature dogs (no doubt the defective offspring of the hot dog, with which twentieth-century Americans were so preoccupied) for the evening meal, followed by passively engaging until midnight in the brutish sport of bull-shooting (the bulls were then processed into a large sausage call bologna)" For such exacting scholarship the good doctor may have won world renown as the foremost authority on twentieth-century*

*English—without having the slightest idea what was actually said! Even worse, imagine the impression his literalism gave his audience of American food and recreational habits! Trying to avoid such error, my search has been for the content of the word rather than its form.*

**Clarence Jordan**
Introduction to *The Cotton Patch Version of Paul's Epistles*

Jesus is the Living Word of God. The library we call the Bible opens our eyes to God's work through the ages, through imperfect people, through inspired writings that we might see and experience Jesus, the Truth and the Life, the Word of God.

It is interesting to note that stories—as opposed to poetry, essays, history, and letters—are often able to transcend language and culture. For instance, the Cinderella story is found in seven to eight hundred versions with the first known example coming from Ninth Century China. Aesop's Fables date back to Aesop's life between 620 and 564 BCE. These fun stories of animal antics have brought wisdom across 2,500 years. Homer's Iliad and Odyssey were told first by storytellers and then written down in the late eighth century or early seventh century BCE. These stories are still heard, studied, and even put on the screen.

Trickster stories have been recorded around the world. Anansi, the spider, from Africa. Coyote from the desert Southwest. Brother Rabbit from Africa via the American South. Jack from Scotland, Ireland, and England via the Appalachians. Jacob from the Old

Testament. We see the small creature or man against large forces, enormous adversaries, giants. David and Goliath stories abound.

The fabric of narrative—with the warp and weft of plot and character—is strong enough to hold a story together across time, culture, and language barriers. My experience in speaking to audiences in different parts of the world displays this principle. I can see when a story is getting across from the facial expressions and body language of the listeners.

In Latvia, I was privileged to work with Kristine Rozefelde who had grown up in Latvia but attended college in the United States. She possessed a firm grasp of the two languages. I used Biblical narratives and folktales to illustrate points in my sermons. Each afternoon before the evening's worship services, Kristine and I would go through my notes. I would tell her the story, and she would talk it through with me:

"No, a porcupine won't work."

"Why?"

"There is no word in Latvian for porcupine."

"Okay, let's make it a hedgehog."

We worked through each tale so she could determine the sense of what I was saying. Thus, the story could be told, and the action could be seen.

The earliest manuscripts of the Hebrew Bible are from Dead Sea Scrolls dating back to 250 BCE. The *oral* tradition predates these scrolls perhaps by thousands of years. The Gospels were not written down until decades after Jesus' earthly life. Stories are hardy and survive, which is why God chose to place so much information and instruction in narrative. Much of Jesus' teaching is in the form of stories.

> *The whole purpose of the Bible, it seems to me, is to convince people to set the written word down in order to become living words in the world for God's sake. For me, this willing conversion of ink back to blood is the full substance of faith.*
>
> **Barbara Brown Taylor**
> Leaving Church

As you read the Bible, listen to and enjoy the stories. Try to see the entire theme as it meanders throughout the library of faith. Listen to the story of the entire Gospel of Luke, or Mark, or Matthew, or John. Listen to the story as it unfolds in Paul's letters to the Corinthians, the Thessalonians, Philemon.

Read the books of the Biblical library as you would other books. Listen to the stories for the Truth they tell. By reading in that manner, you will hear meaning more clearly than by examining chapter and verse.

### *The Gospel of John*

The *Gospel of John* is like no other book in the Bible. Of the four gospels at the beginning of the New Testament, *John* is unlike the other three in that the author tells the story of Jesus in a unique way. Some of the work is shared by the other three but is presented differently.

First and foremost, it is always best to read the whole book. *John* is not a transcription of what Jesus said and did. No one followed Jesus around with a recorder. The gospels are written versions of what people remembered about Jesus' life, his sayings, prayers, actions, healings, and sermons.

> *A Gospel is a retraditioning of the tradition in order to effect a hearing of the Word.*
>
> **Fred Craddock**

When my dad—also named John—pieced puzzles, the point was to see the whole picture by assembling myriad pieces. People often approach scripture by breaking the story into small pieces, a sentence or phrase at a time. The best approach to *John*, however, is to listen to how the writer tells the story of Jesus. When you understand how the writer tells a story, then you are better able to hear the tale being told, the message being sent. It is important to read the entire book.

When I took biology in junior high, we dissected enormous worms and large frogs. It was interesting to see what was inside these creatures and to understand their workings. The exercise taught very little about the life of a frog or worm. Dissecting a story can bring some understanding of the workings of a story, but it often misses the point—not seeing the forest for the trees, to mix many metaphors here.

*John* was written to help the audience meet and know Jesus. We often rush past *John's* work to understand Jesus, Jesus' teachings, or the early church, and when we do, we completely miss what the author is trying to show us. *John* makes it a point to connect seeing and believing several times. The intent of *John's* narrative is for people to see Jesus so that they may believe. (See John 20:30-31).

A literal approach to *John* will not work. The *Gospel of John* is unlike the other three gospels in the way it is written. The writing sounds different. Even the storytelling is distinctive.

> *This is a book in which a child can wade and an elephant can swim.*
>
> **Fred Craddock**
> The Gospels

Those who want to take the scriptures literally will be lost in *John*. If one takes *John* literally, all the wonder and power of Jesus will be missed, because *John* is filled with metaphor, simile, irony, allegory, and story. One must listen to the gospel writer relaying the story. Our common impulse is to explain the scriptures, but to explain a metaphor defeats the purpose of that figure of speech.

> *Metaphors are to be taken seriously and not reduced to a "meaning" or a "truth." They keep our feet on the ground, connected to what is all around us, praying out of our common humanity. Maxine Kumin, a most perceptive poet, writes, "Metaphor is not smaller than life. It mediates between awesome truths. It leaps up*

*from instinctual feeling bearing forth the workable image. Thus in a sense the metaphor is truer than the actual facts.*

**Eugene Peterson**
*Tell It Slant*

In other words, when you dissect a metaphor, it loses its meaning. When you stare at the pieces of the puzzle individually, you cannot see the picture.

Robert Frost was once pressed to explain "Stopping by Woods on a Snowy Evening." Frost asked the questioner if he had read the poem.

"Yes."

"THAT is what I meant."

When this did not seem to satisfy the inquisitor who asked a second time for an explanation, Frost said, "What do you want me to do? Say it in worser English?"

When I was in fourth grade, our teacher, Miss Mary Baker McGee, told us Jack Tales on Friday afternoon to end the week. I loved hearing those wonderful stories. I don't remember much from the fourth grade, but I do remember the adventures of Jack. I later discovered that Miss McGee was using Richard Chase's book *The Jack Tales* as her source. The nerve of that woman tricking us into checking books out from the library! The nerve of *John* tricking people into seeing Jesus in his stories.

Jesus held the attention of his audience. *John* touched the hearts of his audience. When all is said and done, listen to the story. After all, if you have the ears, you will hear.

# Assignment

Read the entire *Gospel of John*. Skip the commentaries and introductions for now. Pick a translation that is easy to read. Find one with no footnotes. (You can do a study later. It is interesting as well).

I enjoy *J.B. Phillips,* Eugene Peterson's *The Message,* Reynolds Price's *The Three Gospels,* but you may use any other version that strikes you. Do not stop along the way and try to analyze the sentences, paragraphs, or individual stories. Listen to the way *John* tells Jesus' story.

# Questions

What jumped out at you as you read the entire book?




What did you see/hear/understand for the first time?

What had you forgotten?

Could you hear *John's* voice in this book about Jesus?

How did you hear *John's* voice?

# CHAPTER TWO
# John as a Storyteller

*John* has a unique storytelling style. In the Synoptic Gospels, Jesus talks about the Kingdom of God (or Kingdom of Heaven), but in *John,* Jesus talks about himself. The word "kingdom" appears more than fifty times in Matthew, though only four times in *John.* The author of *John* approaches the story of Jesus unlike any other of the time. The author writes an autobiography from the perspective of one of Jesus' disciples. The other gospels are more biographical in nature.

Luke began by saying:

*Many people have already applied themselves to the task of compiling an account of the events that have been fulfilled among us. They used what the original eyewitnesses and servants of the word handed down to us. Now, after having investigated everything carefully from the beginning, I have also decided to write a carefully ordered account for you, most honorable Theophilus. I want you to have confidence in the soundness of the instruction you have received.*

**Luke 1:1-4 (CEB)**

In other words, he is saying, "I have done good research on Jesus, and I want to confirm the teachings you have received."

On the other hand, the author of *John* wrote:

> *Then Jesus did many other miraculous signs in his disciples' presence, signs that aren't recorded in this scroll. But these things are written so that you will believe that Jesus is the Christ, God's Son, and that believing, you will have life in his name.*
>
> **John 20:30-31 (CEB)**

In essence, "I could not tell you everything Jesus did, I had to leave some things out, but I want you to know him and understand who he really is."

As Fred Craddock writes in his book *The Gospels:*

> *The author's concern was not to win new converts but to confirm the faith of his own community and to correct the faith of those whose beliefs he regarded as erroneous."*

A few stories are told in all four gospels:

- Jesus in the temple
- The ministry of John the Baptizer
- Feeding of the five thousand
- The Crucifixion
- The Resurrection

Some elements are absent from *John* but present in Matthew, Mark, and Luke:

- Parables
- Jesus' struggles in the wilderness
- Exorcisms
- Ethical instructions

- Messianic secrecy
- Jesus' struggles in Garden of Gethsemane

However, new material also exists in *John* that appears nowhere else in canonical literature. Some new stories of Jesus include:

- The wedding at Cana
- Nicodemus
- The woman at the well
- The healing pool
- The woman caught in adultery
- The raising of Lazarus

Some material is shared between the gospels but is not in the same chronological order. Examples include the cleansing of the temple, the fact that Jesus and John the Baptizer had concurrent ministries instead of sequential work, and Jesus' three trips to Jerusalem for the Passover. Often readers try to reconcile *John's* chronology with that of the other three gospels.

For instance, *Luke* chronicles the story about a large catch of fish as happening early in Jesus' ministry (Luke 5:1-11). *John,* on the other hand, relates a story of a very large catch after the Resurrection (John 21:1-19). Both accounts end with a call to follow Jesus. Many people try to reconcile this discrepancy in the timeline by saying the fishing expeditions occurred twice. This reconciliation attempt is really a red herring. Learn to listen to what *John* is saying about Jesus instead of trying to figure out when an event actually happened.

*John* is a good storyteller. He uses the sequencing episodes to make his point as to who Jesus is. The purpose of the writing is for people to see and believe in Jesus. *John* carefully places the sequence of episodes to make his point. Jesus' angry encounter with moneychangers and merchants on the temple grounds is a good example. Matthew 21:12-13, Mark 11:15-19, and Luke 19:45-48 all locate the "cleansing of the temple" after the Palm Sunday entrance into Jerusalem the last week of Jesus' life. John 2:13-25 places the same episode at the beginning of Jesus' ministry right after the wedding at Cana.

*John* is making a point about Jesus being the temple (see Chapter 6), which permeates his entire story. The other three gospels use this moment as the time when the religious authorities begin plotting against Jesus.

I tell a performance piece about one of my brothers. I want the audience to get a sense of who my brother is and what he has done. Every event in the story actually happened. However, as I tell the story, not all the episodes are in the proper chronological order.

Once, as I told a story about my brother, our sister was in the audience. Afterwards, she said, "That's not the way it happened." I explained that if I had told a certain moment first, it would have been in the correct order, but our brother's identity and his true nature would not have been as obvious. I am much more interested in people coming to know my brother than in understanding the correct timeline of his life.

The author of *John* is more interested in presenting an accurate portrait of Jesus than in delineating a timeline of events. Often, a reader of the Bible might forget that the book is derived from oral traditions of Jesus. Before photography, portrait painters attempted to portray the personality of their subjects in addition to accurately recording the subject's physical features. None of the four gospels are photographs or audio/visual recordings of the life and teachings of Jesus. They are all written versions of a person's or community's memories of Jesus. *John* is perhaps a more impressionistic portrait than the other three, but the gospel remains true to the author's experience and knowledge.

My family speaks in story. I didn't realize it was a different way of expression until I was in elementary school. As I mentioned before, one of my teachers read us *The Jack Tales* by Richard Chase every Friday afternoon. Another teacher read aloud *Hal and Roger Hunt Adventures* by Willard Price. Those books never stayed on the shelves of the school library, because we all wanted to read them over and over.

In the preface of *The Jack Tales,* Chase wrote:

> *In reading these stories, it must be kept constantly in mind that this is an oral tradition.*[8]

Chase went on to give helpful storytelling advice and an interesting look into oral culture.

---

8  Richard Chase, *The Jack Tales,* HMH Books for Young Readers, 2003.

*We pass on this suggestion, based on the advice and the actual practice of our informants, to those parents who find this book and want to enjoy The Jack Tales with their children: Try to tell them without the book. After you have got the drift of any tale, forget the printed page, and tell it as you please. For all true folk traditions have this dynamic appeal. They stick with us, and they grow and change with every individual who receives them.*

*It is only when our old songs and old tales are passing from one human being to another, by word-of-mouth, that they can attain their full fascination. No printed page can create this spell. It is the living word – the sung ballad and the told tale – that holds our attention and reaches our heart.*

**Richard Chase**
The Jack Tales

## John the Teller

Much has been written about the author of the *Gospel of John*. Some propose the writer was John the Disciple, the brother of James and son of Zebedee. Others say it was John the Elder, who lived in Ephesus. Still others attribute the book to a disciple of John the Apostle, the brother of James, or John the Elder. Manuscript evidence is lacking to settle this argument.

Listen to the tone of the work. It sounds like a firsthand account. Perhaps it was passed down orally and was actually written down by a student or descendant of *John's*.

I have admired *John's* writing since before I translated the book as a Greek student. My professor,

Dr. Fred Kellogg, opened my eyes to *John's* artistry. My own thoughts for this book have rattled around in my mind and heart for years. I was talking to my daughter one day about the idea of authorship. Later she sent me a text. It read:

> *John: I won!*
> *Peter: Who's even gonna know?*
> *John (whispers): Everyone will know.*

> *So Peter and the other disciple started for the tomb. Both were running but the other disciple outran Peter and reached the tomb first.*
> **John 20:3-4**

Early in my pastoral work, I visited a member of my new congregation. She was eighty-four in 1984 when I began to visit her. I enjoyed being with her. She had a wonderful memory and told stories well. She was a goldmine of information about the community in which I was serving.

One day she told me she had known her great-grandmother quite well. She then related the story of how, as a child, she and this older woman would sit under a large oak and watch the sheep during the day so her dad and grandfather could do other work on the farm.

"How old was your great-grandmother?" I asked.

"She lived to be one hundred and twelve!" she answered with pride.

"Wow! How old were you when she died?"

"Twelve."

"Twelve?!?"

"Yes, twelve."

Astonished, I did the math. My friend was born in 1900. Her great-grandmother died in 1912 at the age of 112, which meant she was born in 1800 when John Adams was president! I was stunned to realize I was hearing stories only secondhand from a woman whose grandmother was only a teen when Andrew Jackson fought the Battle of New Orleans, an "old" woman of 65 when Abraham Lincoln was assassinated, and someone who had lived through the three wars of the nineteenth century.

Whose stories did I hear? Was I hearing the great-grandmother's stories or were they my friend's stories? The point is, when a person tells another's story, the story is important, not the teller.

The story of Jesus preserved in the *Gospel of John* was first told. The oral tradition treasured the stories of Jesus, both the ones Jesus told and the ones told about Jesus. Today's culture thinks oral tradition is unreliable, because we have relied on print for hundreds of years. However, in an oral culture, information was wisely preserved in stories and songs. Memory was encased in story so it could be carried to the next generation.

In oral cultures, stories are learned and carefully practiced. Singer/storyteller Sheila Kay Adams of Madison County, North Carolina, learned ballads at her granny's knee. With Sheila Kay's knees against those of her granny, her granny sang the first verse, and

Sheila Kay then sang it back to her. Her granny sang the next verse, and then Sheila Kay sang the first verse and the second. Then her granny sang the third verse, and Sheila Kay sang all three verses until she learned the whole ballad. Oral culture carried truth around in narrative vessels.

> If a story is not about the hearer he will not listen.... A great lasting story is about everyone or it will not last. The strange and foreign is not interesting—only the deeply personal.
>
> **John Steinbeck**

Many commentaries and books speak of the identity of *John's* author. The purpose of this work is to look at the storytelling skills of the author. Tradition suggests the author is John, the brother of James, the son of Zebedee, the Apostle, the disciple of Jesus, who wrote this story in his old age as he lived in Ephesus. It is also possible that one who sat with John "knee to knee" learned the story and wrote it down.

The *Gospel of John* has the sound of an eyewitness account, which might explain what is missing, what is present, what is different. Irenaeus, in the later part of the second century, said he had known old Polycarp, who, in turn, had said he was a young student of the old apostle, John, in Ephesus.

The gospel could be the Apostle John's account that came through a student of his—or even a student of an original student. The point remains, the story is John the Apostle's story, just as my parishioner's great-grandmother's story remained the great-grandmother's tale no matter who told it. Today's culture views copyright issues and authorship differently than that of an oral culture. One can become distracted in this debate and not hear what the original author is doing: introducing people to Jesus.

After the poetic prologue (1:1-18), Jesus' story begins not with his birth or baptism but when an unnamed disciple of John the Baptizer meets the Lamb of God, Jesus. The account starts with what the narrator experienced and knew. *John* reads like original material, unlike the synoptics, which obviously share common sources. There is an immediacy to the book of *John*, which explains some of the gaps and new material, for the original teller could not have been everywhere.

Donald Davis, in *Writing as a Second Language*, proposes that our first language is oral. We learn to speak long before we learn to write. Later, we learn to write in order to communicate. We must learn to translate our spoken language onto the page.

Listen to the tone of *John*. Eugene Peterson believed that we use three languages:

- **Language I** is the one we learn first. It is the language of intimacy, or relationship. When we start learning this language, it doesn't even make sense. It is the language of parents and grandparents to an infant: lalalala, goochee-goochee-goo, mamamama, dadadadada. Hear it? It sounds like nonsense on the surface, but it is full of meaning. Peterson said, "The sounds that pass between parent and infant are incredibly rich in meaning, but less than impressive in content."

- **Language II** is the language of information. We start early by identifying the objects in our universe: "light," "finger," "tree," "sky," "toe," "house," "plate," "cup," "milk," "apple." We teach some of this information with songs: "Head, Shoulders, Knees and Toes" or "ABCDEFG." We get oriented to our universe and learn to navigate in it.

- **Language III** is the language of motivation. "We discover early on that words have the power to make things happen, to bring something out of nothing, to move inert figures into purposive action." This is the language we use to sell soap, market cars, and sway political opinion.

*Our culture depends on Languages II and III. We are well schooled in the language that describes the world in which we live. We are well trained in the language that moves people to buy and join and vote. Meanwhile Language I, the language of intimacy, the language that develops relationships of trust, hope, and understanding, languishes. Once we are clear of the cradle we find less and less encouragement to use it. There is a short-lived recovery of Language I in adolescence when we fall in love and spend hours talking on the telephone using words that eavesdroppers characterize as gibberish. But it is the farthest thing from gibberish: the sounds express relationship, they are listening to the sounds of being. These young people are listening to sounds of being; they are practicing adoration, not solving equations or selling soap. When we enter into courtship and marriage we use this language yet again, finding that it is the only language adequate to the reality of our passions and communications. Romantic love extends and deepens it for as long as we have the will to pursue it. But our*

> *will commonly falters, and in the traffic of the everyday and press of making a living, we content ourselves with the required and easier languages of information and motivation. In the early months of parenting, the basic language is relearned and used for a while. At death, if we know we are dying, we will use nothing else. A few people never quit using it—a few lovers, some poets, the saints—but most let it drift into disuse; Walter Wanegrin, Jr. calls this a "vast massacre of neglect."*
>
> *Languages II and III are no less important in the life of faith but if they are not embedded in Language I they become "thin and gaunt."*
>
> **Eugene H. Patterson**<br>*Answering God: The Psalms as Tools for Prayer*

*John* relies on all three languages to tell his story about Jesus. He leans heavily on Language I because he is telling of his own intimate connection to Jesus, the Messiah. *John* is also trying to inform people as to Jesus' true identity while attempting to persuade them to believe in this Jesus. But the bottom line for *John* is his own intimate relationship to this man who embodies God.

# Assignment

- Read again the entire book of *John*. This time, attempt to read it with no agenda. Simply read it as you would any other story. Do not stop to consider meanings. Do not underline or make notes. Simply read *John* as a story.

- Make a chart of the sequence of episodes, a screenplay approach, if you will. It might be fun to draw scenes in sequence.

# Questions

What is one of your favorite books or stories—not counting those in the Bible?

Why is this your favorite? What do you like about it?

What is your favorite book in the Bible?

Why is it your favorite?

What do you like best about the *Gospel of John?*

Do you like the *Gospel of John* more, less, or about the same as the other gospels?

CHAPTER THREE

# Weaving the Tapestry
## The Art of *John's* Storytelling

As mentioned in the previous chapter, *John* skillfully intertwines Language I into Languages II and III. *John* also uses many storytelling techniques as deftly as the weaver uses weft and warp or the quilter uses scraps, needles, and thread. A few techniques of the storyteller are as follows:

- Plot
- Characters
- Dialogue/Conversation
- Metaphor
- Allusion
- Irony
- Details

*John* was not written to be read privately, individually. *John* was intended to be read aloud to a house church. For the original audience, the *Gospel of John* would not have been read as text to study but heard and experienced as a story or set of stories presented orally.

## Plot

Many people mistakenly equate a memory with a story. Memories are the raw material of which stories are made. Memories are the events and people remembered from our past. A story includes memories but is arranged into a plot with main characters, minor characters, and a setting.

The entire book of *John* is summarized in the Prologue (John 1:1-18), but most specifically, "The Word became flesh and made his home among us. We have seen his glory, glory like that of a father's only son, full of grace and truth" (1:14, CEB). The Word came to his own, whom he had created, and was rejected, while Jesus' followers saw him in his glory for who he really was and is.

> *In every story we meet a main character who lives in a clearly described time and place. There may be other characters, but the main character stands out from all of them and is usually who has something to learn. The narrator may also be the main character.*
>
> *Once we meet the main character, we very soon begin to get the sense that trouble is coming. We begin to see some of the main character's flaws of judgment and/or information and we know that a crisis is on the way, though we do not yet know what it is.*
>
> *Now the crisis comes. We watch the main character enter and go through all the throes of the critical event.*
>
> *In the process of living through the crisis, the main character either gets help or learns something new which enables survival of the crisis. This help or*

*learning is something which could never have been acquired apart from struggling through this particular critical event.*

*Once this new learning or insight has been acquired by the main character, life is, in some way, never the same. The end of the story often comes when a recurrence of the same crisis is successfully met or when there is a "forever after that" affirmation of some sort.*[9]

One way to look at the plot of John is:

- **Main Character** – The Word; come to know Jesus in signs and his own "I Am" words.
- **Trouble Coming** – Hints; the Jewish leaders, the blind man, Lazarus
- **Crisis** – The Cross
- **Insight** – The Garden
- **Affirmation** – Thomas and Peter in the final chapters, Chapters 20 and 21

Another way to see the plot is:

- **Prologue**
- **Jesus' Self-Revelation to the World and Students**
- **Jesus' Prayer**
- **Jesus' Death**
- **Epilogue**

---

9  Donald Davis, *Telling Your Own Stories*, August House, p. 37.

Many commentaries offer outlines and plot lines. Try to discern the plot of *John* from your reading.

## John's Cast of Characters

Every good story has characters. Obviously, the main character in *John's* story is Jesus, the Messiah. *John* tells you that outright from the beginning and never lets you forget it. He also leaves clues and allusions and employs a large cast of lesser characters to tell Jesus' story. Some of these characters appear several times, and others only make brief appearances and are gone. Some are named while others are nameless. Some have nicknames or qualifiers—Andrew, Simon Peter's brother (poor guy, always Simon's brother, obviously not a first child); Joseph of Arimathea; Thomas, the one called the Twin; the other disciple; the mother of Jesus (never Mary and only appears twice, once near the beginning and once near the end); the sons of Zebedee; and others.

*John* does not give a list of Jesus' disciples as other sources do (Matthew 10:1-4, Mark 3:16-19, Luke 6:14-16, and Acts 1:13-14). *John* does refer to the Twelve (6:67), but *John* never gives twelve names as the ones. There are a few disciples who are important but nameless. This could be out of modesty or a storytelling device (see Meditations – Breakfast on the Beach on page 183).

Notice how *John* populates Jesus' story with many different types of people. Some characters get more "airtime" than others. For instance, Peter, Nicodemus, the woman at the well, the man born blind, Judas (Simon Iscariot's son), to name a few. Some only appear once, and we never hear of them again. Mary Magdalene comes at the very end of the story in a span of only three days. Others are cameos, existing in the story for only a moment. (Malchus; Judas, not Iscariot; Joseph of Arimathea; Sons of Zebedee; Barabbas; his mother's sister; Mary, the wife of Clopas).

What do the characters tell you about Jesus? *John* weaves in various individuals so you can better see Jesus. Even during the night with Nicodemus, Jesus is seen in a brighter light. Try to look at the people in *John's* story for what they reveal.

## Disciples

- **Andrew:** (1:40-45; 6:8; and 12:22), always referred to as Simon Peter's brother
- **Simon Peter/Cephas:** (1:40-42; 6:68; 13:6-37; 18:10-27; 20:2-6; and 21:2-18)
- **Philip:** (1:43-48; 6:5-7; 12:21-22; and 14:8-9)
- **Nathanael:** (1:45-49 and 21:2), only appears twice and is not on any other lists
- **Sons of Zebedee:** (21:2), the names James and John are not mentioned in *John*
- **The Twelve:** (6:67), the only mention of Twelve Disciples
- **Judas, Simon Iscariot's son:** (6:71;12:4; 13:2,26,29; and 18:2-3,5)
- **Thomas/Didymus:** (11:16; 14:5; 20:24,26,27; and 21:2)
- **The Disciple Whom Jesus Loved/Beloved:** (13:23;19:26;21:7)

- **Judas, not Iscariot:** (14:22)
- **The Other/Another Disciple:** (18:15;20:2;20:3;20:4;21:20)
- **Joseph of Arimathea, a disciple of Jesus:** (19:38)

## Women

- **Jesus' mother:** (2:3,5,12, wedding at Cana) (19:25–27 at the Cross)
- **Woman of Samaria at the well:** (4:4-42) First to Hear "I Am"
- **Woman caught in adultery:** (8:3-11)
- **Mary, sister of Lazarus & Martha:** (11:1-45, raising of Lazarus and 12:1-8, anointing of Jesus)
- **Martha, sister of Lazarus & Mary:** (11:1-39, raising of Lazarus)
- **Woman at the gate:** (18:16, confronts Peter)
- **Jesus' mother's sister:** (19:25 at the Cross), possibly Mary, wife of Clopas
- **Mary, wife of Clopas:** (19:25 at the Cross), possibly Mary's sister
- **Mary Magdalene:** (19:25 at the Cross) (20:1,2, finds Empty Tomb), (20:11-18, sees Jesus)

## Others

- **John the Baptizer:** (1:6-8; 1:19-34; 3:22-36; 5:31-46)
- **Nicodemus:** (3:1-21; 7:50-52; 19:38-42)
- **Woman of Samaria at the well:** (4:4-52)

- **Royal official:** (4:46-54)
- **Sick man at Bethsaida:** (5:1-18)
- **Woman caught in adultery:** (8:1-11)
- **Man born blind:** (9:1-41)
- **Lazarus, Mary, and Martha:** (11:1-46 and 12:1-9)
- **Malchus, high priest's servant who lost ear to Peter at arrest of Jesus:** (18:10)
- **Pilate:** (18:28-19:16 and 19:16-24; 19:38-42)
- **Annas, a chief priest:** (18:13,24)
- **Caiaphas, a chief priest:** (11:49-52; 18:13-28)
- **Barabbas:** (18:38-40), an off-stage character.
- **His mother's sister/Mary, wife of Clopas:** (19:25-27)
- **Mary Magdalene:** (19:25; 20:1,2; 20:11-18), only appears at the end of the story
- **The Jews, Jewish officials, and the Pharisees:** (many appearances!)

## Dialogue/Conversations

Another thread storytellers use to stitch together a story is conversation or dialogue. Galileo used dialogue to describe his thoughts and discoveries on the nature of a heliocentric solar system. The truth of the physics lay in mathematics—a language poorly understood by most. So, Galileo wrote *The Dialogue Concerning the Two Chief World Systems (Dialogo sopra i due massimi sistemi del mondo)*. First published in 1632, the work was so well read and understood that it was put on the Index of Forbidden Books by 1633. (Another method Galileo employed was to issue the book in Italian instead of Latin.) One reason Galileo's work was banned was because he presented the truth in the form of a conversation instead of mathematical formulas. His three characters presented the arguments for the Ptolemaic system, the Copernican system, and a voice of reason that mediated the discussion.

Plays are mostly conversations. Usually, you don't hear what a character is thinking. Alas, Hamlet speaks to dead Yorick, but even in that example, Hamlet's soliloquy is a one-sided conversation with a dead man. The Stage Manager in Eugene O'Neill's Our Town is a narrator who sets up the conversations you hear between the characters.

Conversation is a time-honored storytelling method. When I tell the most outlandish Appalachian tall tales, I put them in the mouth of a mountain teller who is relating a story to me. The teller is not me, even though I am the one speaking. The teller is someone speaking to me.

*John* uses this device brilliantly. We overhear conversations throughout the entire book. In fact, it would be easy to convert *John's* text into a play or screenplay with very little editing. Just after the poetic prologue, we overhear a conversation between John the Baptizer and others (1:19-34). This is followed by a conversation with Jesus and two of John the Baptizer's students.

And then we are off!

- **The wedding at Cana** – Jesus and his mother (2:1-12)
- **In the temple** – Jesus and the Jewish Leaders in the temple (2:13-21)
- **A night visit** – Jesus and Nicodemus (3:1-21)
- **A debate on cleansing** – John the Baptizer, his disciples, and a "certain Jew" (3:22-36)
- **The woman at the well** – Jesus and an unnamed woman (4:4-42)
- **The second sign** – the healing takes place during the conversation between Jesus and a royal official (4:46-54)
- **A Sabbath healing** – Jesus, a sick man, and Jewish leaders (5:1-18)

Need I go on? The entire book. Look for yourselves. Compare this with the Synoptic Gospels where there is more narration and more monologues from Jesus (as opposed to dialogues).

*John's* usual pattern is Jesus says something, it is misunderstood by the hearer who responds, and then Jesus clarifies. The hearer often speaks what the audience is probably thinking.

- "How can you be born all over again?"
- "You don't have a bucket! You just asked me for water. How are you going to give me water?"
- "What do you mean, 'Do I want to get well?' Of course! But there is nobody to help me." (This is even funny because the one who could help him the most was standing right in front of him!) The original audience probably laughed or smiled at this point.

People like to listen in on other people's conversations. You hear them in restaurants, in grocery store lines, on airplanes, everywhere. Sometimes you only hear half the conversation because the person is on the phone. *John* simply presents Jesus' story in a form that is familiar and interesting.

## METAPHOR

Yet another storytelling tool *John* uses is metaphor. We learned the definition of "metaphor" in our school days.

*Noun*

1. A figure of speech in which a word or phrase is applied to an object or action to which it is not literally applicable.
2. A thing regarded as representative or symbolic of something else, especially something abstract. (Oxford Languages)

I remember a classmate of mine in ninth grade English class. He said, "You mean it's a word that means something it's not?!"

"Yes!"

"Well," he said, "That's just horse s**t!"

"Precisely," I said, "That's a metaphor. It's not actually road apples (another metaphor—see what I did there?), but it means that it is."

My friend just shook his head.

I once heard the physicist Brian Greene in an interview with Terry Gross on NPR's Fresh Air talking about his book *Fabric of the Cosmos*. It was a book about astrophysics and cosmology, a topic that is mostly complicated mathematics. However, he used metaphor to describe the mathematical realities of the universe with phrases like "string theory," "tears in the fabric," and "fabric of the cosmos."[10]

Emily Dickinson used metaphor in her poem "Tell It Slant," where she essentially said Truth is too difficult to see. You must use metaphor and story to get Truth across.

> *Tell all the truth but tell it slant —*
> *Success in Circuit lies*
> *Too bright for our infirm Delight*
> *The Truth's superb surprise*
> *As Lightning to the Children eased*
> *With explanation kind*
> *The Truth must dazzle gradually*
> *Or every man be blind —*
>
> **Emily Dickinson**

Heather Frost tells a wonderful rendition of a Jewish folktale entitled "Naked Truth." It is a fun verse describing how hard it is to look at naked truth.

*John's* work is full of metaphor, as are Jesus' words and actions. They include examples such as these:

---

10 *Fresh Air*, National Public Radio, March 2004.

- The Word
- The Lamb of God
- The Bread
- The Good Shepherd
- The Gate
- The True Vine
- The Light

> *"Metaphor, after all, is neither the candle nor the wick, but the burning."*
>
> **Thomas Hobstadt**

## ALLUSION

Still another thread in our amazing Johannine story of Jesus is "allusion," which is defined as follows:

*Noun:*

An expression designed to call something to mind without mentioning it explicitly; an indirect or passing reference. (Oxford Languages)

Again, start in the first chapter of *John*. The very first words, "In the beginning" are an allusion to Genesis 1:1. From the very first words, *John* tells you he is framing the story of Jesus in the entire creation.

Matthew begins Jesus' story with a genealogy

(starting with Abraham) and then gives an account of Jesus' birth. Mark begins with a quotation from the book of Isaiah, next a reference to John the Baptizer's teaching, and then Jesus' baptism. Luke writes an introductory paragraph about his sources and then moves to John the Baptizer's birth. Luke goes on to relate the events surrounding Jesus' birth from Mary's perspective and finally gets to Jesus' genealogy in the fourth chapter but relates Jesus to Adam who was "the son of God" (Luke 4:38).

From the beginning, *John* connects Jesus' story to the entire universe, to creation itself. In John 1:14, the very word "tented" or "lived among us" is an allusion to the tabernacle in the wilderness wanderings of the people of Israel.

John the Baptizer referred to Jesus as "the Lamb of God," which is an allusion to God supplying a lamb for Abraham as a stand-in for Isaac (Genesis 22:1-19) and the lamb to the slaughter of Isaiah (Isaiah 53:7). In John 1:51, Jesus alludes to the Jacob story by mentioning a stairway with angels going up and down to heaven and then makes the stairway a metaphor for himself.

The serpent lifted in the wilderness (mentioned by Jesus to Nicodemus) is an allusion to Numbers 21:8-9. The setting for the woman at the well is Samaria, which is an allusion to where the first temple stood at Mt. Gerizim (Deuteronomy 11:29).

As you can see, you cannot read through the book of *John* without tripping over allusions to Hebrew scripture. At times, *John* tells a story using an image or object from another episode already told. The charcoal fire in 21:9 recalls the charcoal fire of 18:18 so that you connect Peter's betrayal with his forgiveness.

There are mentions of bread and wine in various episodes. These allude to the Lord's Supper, whose words of institution are oddly missing from *John*, although *John's* telling may be the most sacramental of the four gospels.

There are plenty of commentaries and books that cover this topic of Hebrew Scripture allusions and quotes in *John*. One way to find allusions is to read footnotes in a study Bible. A good study Bible has scripture references in a central or marginal column or in notes at the bottom of the page. A good online concordance or commentary will help you find Hebrew Scripture references in the New Testament.

## IRONY

*John* often masterfully stitches with irony. The definition of irony is stated below:

*Noun*

1. The expression of one's meaning by using language that normally signifies the opposite, typically for humorous or emphatic effect.
2. A state of affairs or an event that seems deliberately contrary to what one expects and is often amusing as a result.

3. A literary technique, originally used in Greek tragedy, by which the full significance of a character's words or actions are clear to the audience or reader although unknown to the character.[11]

In irony, there are always two levels. This is *John's* style. He writes on multiple levels, particularly when he employs irony. My Greek teacher, Dr. Frederick Kellogg, once said that if *John* uses a word that has more than one meaning, *John* usually means all of them.

A few examples of irony in *John* are the following:

1. 4:15 – "The woman said to him, 'Sir, give me this water, so that I will never be thirsty and will never need to come here to draw water!'" The woman asks for water from the person who is Living Water. However, at the end of Jesus' life, the Living Water cries out that he is thirsty (19:28).

2. 6:32-35 – "They said, "Sir, give us this bread all the time!" The crowd asks for bread from the one who fed the five thousand and who actually is the bread of life.

3. 11:47-53 – "You don't know anything! You don't see that it is better for you that one man die for the people rather than the whole nation be destroyed." The high priest Caiaphas says this to mean Jesus needs to be executed to preserve Israel from the Romans, not understanding that Jesus' death would be for all people.

---

[11] *Oxford Languages,* https://languages.oup.com/.

4. 18:33-38 – "'What is truth?' Pilate asked." The whole conversation drips with irony. Are you a king? What is truth? The King of Kings, the Truth was standing right in front of him. People hearing this read aloud probably giggled.

There is much more! Only the blind man sees while those with sight are blind. The mourners and sisters cry and so does Jesus at Lazarus' death while the resurrection is standing right before them. You get a sense that *John* threads irony throughout the narrative.

## DETAILS

> *God is in the details.*
>
> **Ludwig Mies van der Rohe**
> Architect

In telling a story, details are important. Too many details, however, can slow down a story or distract from the main point. The best storytellers use few details, leaving the bulk of the work to the imagination of the audience. For instance, Jesus uses few adjectives in his parables within the Synoptics, and the parables are brief.

*John* uses details judiciously. If there is a detail, it means something. In fact, when you hear a detail, especially one that does not seem important, slow down. Try to hear what is being said. Below are a few examples of details in *John* that carry meaning.

- **"Tented"**(1:14) – The word that is translated "lived among us" is originally "pitched a tent" or "tented" among us. The tabernacle was the Tent of Meeting (See the Chapter Six).

- **Four p.m.** (1:39) – An odd detail. A ring of firsthand authenticity but also the memory of one who could never forget the encounter with Jesus.

- **Six jars holding 20 to 30 gallons each**—used for the Jewish cleansing rites (2:6). The number six denotes near perfection but slightly less than the perfection, signified by the number seven. The Law required presenting oneself "clean" before the Lord God. There are huge jars holding lots of water. An abundance of water to cleanse turns into an abundance of fine wine.

- **Night** – (3:2) Nicodemus comes at night. The author of *John* came at four o'clock in the afternoon. Nicodemus meets Jesus in the dark. Did Nicodemus seek Jesus when no one else could see him? When no one else would know? Did Nicodemus think that God works amazingly at night?

- **Noon** (4:6) – Midday at a well. Most people drew water in the morning and evening. Is the woman seeking the same anonymity that Nicodemus was seeking? So, noon at the well when no one else was around?

- **Recline/Grass** (6:10) – Jesus said, "'Have them recline.' There was plenty of grass there." We often miss the "recline" detail because of inadequate translations. The word is the word used for the position in which one enjoys a banquet. We tend to sit at a banquet; thus, it is most often rendered "sit." The problem is, we also sit for snacks, breakfast, lunch, and picnics. The detail here is lying down in grass.

- **Charcoal fire** (18:18 and 21:9) – A very odd detail. Why not the word for fire? A charcoal fire has a distinct smell. *John* the storyteller evokes the smell of two moments in Peter's life.
- **One hundred and fifty-three fish** (21:11) – Many commentaries have discussed the significance of the number 153. It could be as simple as an eyewitness detail which basically slipped out: "I've never seen that many fish! There were 153!"
- **Fish and bread** (6:11 and 21:13) – Twice Jesus feeds with fish and bread. A nice connection of two moments when the disciples see Jesus in a new way. The second mention evokes, or alludes, to the first.

Some details were included to make a point about Jesus. *John* wrote in a time when Gnostics and Docetists were teaching that Jesus was a spirit and only appeared to be human. Special knowledge was required to be one of Jesus' people. *John* adds in details that show otherwise. For example:

- **Tired, thirsty, and hungry with the woman at the well** (4:4-41)
- **Spitting in the dirt** (9:6)
- **Weeping at Lazarus' tomb** (11:35)
- **Washing feet** (13:1-20)
- **Crucifixion** (19:16-30)

The Word became flesh and blood. The Word was not an idea or a spirit that floated around. Can you spot other interesting details? What could the author be hinting at or showing?

Also, look for repeated words or phrases. A storyteller drives home points with repetition. In a work that is all about knowing Jesus by seeing him and his signs, it is significant that "Come and see" appears frequently (1:39; 1:46; 4:29; 9:37; 11:34, to name a few). The first usage of "come and see" is actually Jesus' invitation to discipleship—almost as if to say, Don't take my word for it. Come and see.

The Synoptic Gospels tell the story of Jesus. In *John*, Jesus IS the story.

> *This, perhaps, is why John is the favorite Gospel of so many Christian believers. More than any other it draws the readers into the ancient story, assuring all who believed that they are God's children, born not from blood nor from human desire or passion, but born from God" (John 1:12-13). Its legacy is nothing less than a new birth, a promise of eternal life that begins not at death, nor even at the coming of God's kingdom, but here and now.*
>
> **J. Ramsey Michaels**[12]

Many commentaries consider the scholarship of text and form criticism to discuss when and where the book of *John* was written. Understanding why *John* approaches the story of Jesus in the manner he does can be helpful. Narrative criticism approaches the text as story-narrative-first. I would argue that this is the way *John* was written and intended to be heard. This is not to say that text and form criticism are not needed

---

12 J. Ramsey Michaels in CEB "Introduction to the Gospel of John," NT, p. 168.

or important. They are wonderful for digging deeper and deeper into the text. We see this in studying, for example, William Shakespeare, Robert Frost, Ernest Hemingway, Lee Smith, or Barbara Kingsolver. No matter the writer, it is best to first listen to what they actually say in the text. Next, listen to how they say it. Then move to closer inspection.

> *Story enlists our imagination to grasp more than our immediate feelings and surroundings—other lives, other circumstances, other possibilities. Once we are free of being stuck in the mud of our sinful, self-absorbed, self-contained 'miry clay' of ego, our imaginations can be a catalyst for faith that the Spirit uses to create something out of nothing, the assurance of things hoped for, the conviction of "things not seen...that the worlds were prepared by the word of God, so that what is seen was made from things that are not visible" (Hebrews 11:1-3).*
>
> **Eugene Peterson**
> *Tell It Slant*, p. 116

A story shows so that the audience sees. In the Synoptics, Jesus calls his students to be servants. In *John*, we see Jesus kneel as a servant and wash his students' feet. *John* tells the story of Jesus' life so that you can see him as *John* himself did.

## Assignment

Read the entire book of John. Try to read a version that does not have chapters and verses. Just read straight through and listen to the book as a complete story.

## Questions

What strikes you? What jumps out at you?

What did you hear that you had never noticed before?

What questions do you have?

What did the storyteller repeat in order to get your attention?

What details leaped off the page?

Create an outline of the entire book. What was the plot?

Who were your favorite characters?

## CHAPTER FOUR
## I Am

# Ἐγώ εἰμι

The windows in my home church, Signal Crest United Methodist, are a wonder to behold. I don't know who designed or made them, but they are amazing. As a youth, I knew they were special and that not every church had windows like ours. The sanctuary walls, back to front, floor to ceiling, were stained glass. The western side caught the afternoon light and depicted four scenes of the Trinity. Even as a kid, I thought it was funny to have four windows for the Trinity: God the Creator, Jesus Incarnate, Jesus Resurrected, and the Holy Spirit.

The opposite side of the room glowed in the morning light. The four scenes were called the "I Am" windows. Symbols in these panels showed I Am the light, I Am the bread of life, I Am the good shepherd, and I Am the true vine.

When I asked our pastor, Walter Smalley, what the windows meant, he said, "Read the *Gospel of John*."

One of the bold threads running throughout *John* is "I Am." Oddly, we often miss this thread as we read through English versions of *John*. The poetic I Ams get lost in the translation.

Often the phrase Ἐγώ εἰμι (Ego eimi) is rendered as "It is I," a grammatically correct phrase in English. Sometimes I hear it as what Ernest T. Bass used to say on the old Andy Griffith shows: "It's me. It's me. It's Ernest T." Throughout *John*, when we read some English versions, Jesus is saying, "It is I," or even, "It's me!"

However, Jesus is saying something much more important, much deeper. In the original language, the early audience would have heard the "I Am."

Another thread in the tapestry of *John* is the teller's attempt to weave in themes and thoughts from the book of Exodus. In Exodus 3, Moses encounters God in a burning bush. Through the bush, God calls Moses to go to Pharoah and demand that God's people be set free. When Moses protests, God basically says, "Go back and do this!" Moses protests again by saying, "When I go back, who should I say sent me? They are going to ask me what your name is. What am I supposed to say?"

> *But Moses said to God, "If I now come to the Israelites and say to them, 'The God of your ancestors has sent me to you,' they are going to ask me, 'What's this God's name?' What am I supposed to say to them?"*
>
> *God said to Moses, "I Am Who I Am. So say to the Israelites, 'I Am has sent me to you.'" God continued, "Say to the Israelites, 'The Lord, the God of your ancestors, Abraham's God, Isaac's God, and Jacob's God, has sent me to you.' This is my name forever; this is how all generations will remember me.*
>
> **Exodus 3:13-15 (CEB)**

"This is my name forever; this is how all generations will remember me." God's name was considered sacred. God's name was protected by the Israelites. You didn't go carelessly tossing God's real name around.

> *Do not use the Lord your God's name as if it were of no significance; the Lord won't forgive anyone who uses his name that way.*
>
> **Exodus 20:7 (CEB)**

Even when the scriptures were being read aloud, one did not utter God's name. The reader would substitute the word "Lord" when they saw יהוה—Yahweh. In fact, when the scriptures were originally written in Hebrew, only consonants were used. Centuries later, in the Diaspora of the Jews, rabbis feared that people would lose the ability to read and understand Hebrew, so they added the vowels into the text. Instead of recopying every text, they "pointed" the text. Scribes used dots and small lines above and below the consonants to indicate the vowels.

Scribes kept the Third Commandment in mind. Instead of adding the correct vowels for Yahweh, they added the vowels for Lord (Adonai) to remind the reader to not say God's name aloud but to instead say "Lord." When the vowels were added in this manner, the word became "Jehovah."

This is how careful the Jewish faith was in using (or not using) God's name. "I Am Who I AM," "I Will Be Who I Will Be," or "I Am."

The first time we hear the phrase "I Am" in *John*,

the fourth chapter outlines Jesus' encounter with the Samaritan woman in John 4:4-26 (CEB):

*Jesus had to go through Samaria. He came to a Samaritan city called Sychar, which was near the land Jacob had given to his son Joseph. Jacob's well was there. Jesus was tired from his journey, so he sat down at the well. It was about noon.*

*A Samaritan woman came to the well to draw water. Jesus said to her, "Give me some water to drink." His disciples had gone into the city to buy him some food.*

*The Samaritan woman asked, "Why do you, a Jewish man, ask for something to drink from me, a Samaritan woman?" (Jews and Samaritans didn't associate with each other.)*

*Jesus responded, "If you recognized God's gift and who is saying to you, 'Give me some water to drink,' you would be asking him and he would give you living water."*

*The woman said to him, "Sir, you don't have a bucket and the well is deep. Where would you get this living water? You aren't greater than our father Jacob, are you? He gave this well to us, and he drank from it himself, as did his sons and his livestock."*

*Jesus answered, "Everyone who drinks this water will be thirsty again, but whoever drinks from the water that I will give will never be thirsty again. The water that I give will become in those who drink it a spring of water that bubbles up into eternal life."*

*The woman said to him, "Sir, give me this water, so that I will never be thirsty and will never need to come here to draw water!"*

*Jesus said to her, "Go, get your husband, and come back here."*

*The woman replied, "I don't have a husband."*

*"You are right to say, 'I don't have a husband,'" Jesus*

*answered. "You've had five husbands, and the man you are with now isn't your husband. You've spoken the truth."*

*The woman said, "Sir, I see that you are a prophet. Our ancestors worshiped on this mountain, but you and your people say that it is necessary to worship in Jerusalem."*

*Jesus said to her, "Believe me, woman, the time is coming when you and your people will worship the Father neither on this mountain nor in Jerusalem. You and your people worship what you don't know; we worship what we know because salvation is from the Jews. But the time is coming—and is here!—when true worshipers will worship in spirit and truth. The Father looks for those who worship him this way. God is spirit, and it is necessary to worship God in spirit and truth."*

*The woman said, "I know that the Messiah is coming, the one who is called the Christ. When he comes, he will teach everything to us."*

*Jesus said to her, "**I Am**—the one who speaks with you."*

In this story, Jesus claims the I Am for himself. Herein lies a large departure from the Synoptics where Jesus did not often use that phrase and, in fact, sometimes asked the disciples or others to not mention who he is. The writer of *John,* on the other hand, wants to make sure that hearers of his work understand who Jesus really is. Jesus is the I Am, God's Word in the flesh.

Essentially, Jesus said to the Samaritan woman at the well, "Don't worry about where to worship God or where the true temple is. I Am is due your worship. I Am is the one for whom the temple was built. You are standing in the presence of I Am."

The I Am thread continues in Chapter Six. Jesus and the disciples have gone away into the wilderness. The crowds have followed them to a lonely place. There Jesus fed the crowd with the meager resources of five barley loaves and two small fish. After this amazing meal with a lot left over, the disciples recrossed the lake. They left without Jesus.

> *When evening came, Jesus' disciples went down to the lake. They got into a boat and were crossing the lake to Capernaum. It was already getting dark and Jesus hadn't come to them yet. The water was getting rough because a strong wind was blowing. When the wind had driven them out for about three or four miles, they saw Jesus walking on the water. He was approaching the boat and they were afraid. He said to them, "I Am. Don't be afraid." Then they wanted to take him into the boat, and just then the boat reached the land where they had been heading.*
> **John 6:16-21 (CEB)**

In the chaos of a storm when the wind was driving the boat, the disciples saw someone walking toward them. Imagine their fear at seeing a ghost or spirit (after all, the word for spirit, wind, and breath are all the same in Greek and Hebrew). As in many encounters throughout the scriptures with the Almighty, the messenger said, "Don't be afraid." The difference this time is the use of the divine name, I Am. "I Am. Don't be afraid." Jesus, the I Am, in person delivered them from the chaos of the storm. Jesus brought them safely to shore.

In Genesis 1:2, "The earth was without shape or form, it was dark over the deep sea, and God's wind (spirit, breath) swept over the waters." Then God spoke creation into being. *John* tells the amazing story of Jesus while referencing the early part of scriptures. (Remember how *John* begins?)

Jesus claimed to be the bread of life by saying, "I Am the bread of life." This caused a stir. After this exchange, many disciples said, "This is too much for me. Let's get out of here." Jesus was using the sacred name for himself. This was going too far.

> *At this, many of his disciples turned away and no longer accompanied him. Jesus asked the Twelve, "Do you also want to leave?" Simon Peter answered, "Lord, where would we go? You have the words of eternal life. We believe and know that you are God's holy one."*
>
> **John 6:66-69 (CEB)**

I like *John's* use of language in this passage. Peter's response to Jesus saying "I Am" is "You are." It is here that Peter confessed his confidence in Jesus as the I Am. Peter said, "There is no one else like you. I mean, where would we go?" This same confession will appear again in response to other words and signs of Jesus.

The next time Jesus claims the divine name is in Chapter 8. He was talking to the crowd, and then the Pharisees engaged in a conversation with questions. Jesus challenges their beliefs: "If you don't believe that **I Am**, you will die in your sins."

Jesus is very clear as to who he is. The Pharisees even ask after this pronouncement, "Who are you?" And Jesus clarifies. *John* leaves no doubt as to Jesus' identity by sprinkling the **I Ams** throughout the book.

He said to them, "You are from below; I'm from above. You are from this world; I'm not from this world. This is why I told you that you would die in your sins. If you don't believe that **I Am**, you will die in your sins."

"Who are you?" they asked.

*Jesus replied, "I'm exactly who I have claimed to be from the beginning. I have many things to say in judgment concerning you. The one who sent me is true, and what I have heard from him I tell the world." They didn't know he was speaking about his Father. So, Jesus said to them, "When the Human One is lifted up, then you will know that I Am. Then you will know that I do nothing on my own, but I say just what the Father has taught me. He who sent me is with me. He doesn't leave me by myself, because I always do what makes him happy." While Jesus was saying these things, many people came to believe in him.*

**John 8:23-30 (CEB)**

After Jesus' entry into Jerusalem, he shared a meal with his disciples at which he washed their feet. In this moment, the Great I Am, the Word who became flesh, the enlivened Tabernacle of God knelt to display the true nature of Yahweh, the I Am (See Philippians 2:6-11).

*You call me "Teacher" and "Lord," and you speak correctly, because I am. If I, your Lord and teacher, have washed your feet, you too must wash each other's feet. I have given you an example: Just as I have done, you also must do. I assure you, servants aren't greater than their master, nor are those who are sent greater than the one who sent them. Since you know these things, you will be happy if you do them. I'm not speaking about all of you. I know those whom I've chosen. But this is to fulfill the scripture, The one who eats my bread has turned against me.*

*I'm telling you this now, before it happens, so that when it does happen you will believe that **I Am**.*

**John 13:13-19 (CEB)**

Our author told of Jesus' true identity over and over. But so the audience will have no doubts or misunderstanding, one more moment is shown. This time it is in the garden after the Last Supper. Judas led soldiers and guards to arrest Jesus.

*After he said these things, Jesus went out with his disciples and crossed over to the other side of the Kidron Valley. He and his disciples entered a garden there. Judas, his betrayer, also knew the place because Jesus often gathered there with his disciples. Judas brought a company of soldiers and some guards from the chief priests and Pharisees. They came there carrying lanterns, torches, and weapons. Jesus knew everything that was to happen to him, so he went out and asked, "Who are you looking for?"*

*They answered, "Jesus the Nazarene."*

*He said to them, "**I Am**." (Judas, his betrayer, was standing with them.) When he said, "**I Am**," they shrank back and fell to the ground. He asked them again, "Who are you looking for?"*

*They said, "Jesus the Nazarene."*

*Jesus answered, "I told you, '**I Am**.' If you are looking for me, then let these people go." This was so that the word he had spoken might be fulfilled: "I didn't lose anyone of those whom you gave me."*

**John 18:1-9 (CEB)**

In the garden, we hear I Am, I Am, I Am. And lest you miss the point, consider the reaction of the guards and soldiers. Jesus asked, "Who are you looking for?" They answered, "Jesus the Nazarene." If Jesus had simply answered, "I am he," they would have grabbed him and been off. But Jesus didn't say, "I am he" or "It is I." What Jesus said was, "**I Am**." He used the name of God, and the soldiers shrank back and fell to the ground! Yiiii! Blasphemy! They could not believe that anyone would say that, and they reacted. It is at this moment in *John's* story that Jesus claims the title for himself for the last time. The name is repeated three times just so *John's* audience does not miss the point. (When I was in school if a professor related something three times, I knew it was important and would be on the test!) This is important to *John's* telling of Jesus' story. Jesus is God embodied, Emmanuel. Jesus is the ultimate sacrificial Lamb. Jesus is the Word in the world. Jesus is the I Am.

Just so the original audience heard Jesus as the **I Am**, *John* used the device of metaphor. The great statement of "**I Am**" echoes throughout the work in metaphors—all designed to reveal who Jesus actually is. This is a place where biblical literalism does not work. To take the I am statements literally is to miss the point and the power of the images. I am the Bread, I am the Light, I am the Gate, I am the Good Shepherd, I am the Resurrection and the Life, I am the Way, the Truth, and the Life, I am the True Vine.

| John 6:35 | I am the bread |
| --- | --- |
| John 8:12 | I am the light |
| John 10:7 | I am the gate |
| John 10:11 | I am the good shepherd |
| John 11:25 | I am the resurrection and the life |
| John 14:6 | I am the way, the truth, and the life |
| John 15:1 | I am the true vine |

Another way *John* uses **I Am** is in the negative: I am not. In the opening poem of the prologue, John the Baptizer speaks out to his own identity and the identity of the Messiah.

> *This is John's testimony when the Jewish leaders in Jerusalem sent priests and Levites to ask him, "Who are you?"*
>
> *John confessed (he didn't deny but confessed), "**I'm not** the Christ."*
>
> *They asked him, "Then who are you? Are you Elijah?"*
>
> *John said, "**I'm not**."*
>
> *"Are you the prophet?"*
>
> *John answered, "**No**."*
>
> *They asked, "Who are you? We need to give an answer to those who sent us. What do you say about yourself?"*
>
> *John replied,*
>
> *"I am a voice crying out in the wilderness,*
> *  Make the Lord's path straight,*
> *  just as the prophet Isaiah said."*
>
> **John 1:19-23 (CEB)**

In some of the first sentences of the book of *John*, just after declaring the Word became alive in the flesh

(John 1:14), *John* the author makes it clear that John the Baptizer is not for whom everyone was waiting. John the Baptizer said, "I am not!" "I am not!" "No, I'm not the one."

Near the end of the book, the author does the same thing. Listen to how Peter responds in the courtyard while following Jesus from a distance.

> *Simon Peter and another disciple followed Jesus. Since that disciple was known to the high priest, he went with Jesus into the courtyard of the high priest, but Peter was standing outside at the gate. So the other disciple, who was known to the high priest, went out, spoke to the woman who guarded the gate, and brought Peter in. The woman said to Peter, "You are not also one of this man's disciples, are you?" He said, "**I am not**." Now the slaves and the police had made a charcoal fire because it was cold, and they were standing around it and warming themselves. Peter also was standing with them and warming himself.*
>
> **John 18:13-18 (NRSV)**

> *Now Simon Peter was standing and warming himself. They asked him, "You are not also one of his disciples, are you?" He denied it and said, "**I am not**." One of the slaves of the high priest, a relative of the man whose ear Peter had cut off, asked, "Did I not see you in the garden with him?" Again Peter **denied** it, and at that moment the cock crowed.*
>
> **John 18:25-27 (NRSV)**

The Synoptics phrase Peter's denial differently. In Matthew, Peter says, "I don't know the man." Mark says, "I don't know what you're talking about," and "I don't know the man you are talking about." Luke wrote it as, "Woman, I don't know him!" "Man, I'm not!" and "Man,

I don't know what you are talking about!"

*John,* on the other hand, ends with Peter using the negative of Jesus' I Ams: "I am not!" "I am not!" "I am not!" This artful way of remembering this part of the story of Jesus leaves no doubt as to who Jesus is.

The **I Am** becomes human. The entire book of *John* is about the I Am pitching a tent, being the tabernacle among us (1:14). The author of *John* skillfully stitches the I Am thread throughout the narrative to make it is obvious that Jesus is I Am. The writer does not want there to be any doubt. "These are written so that you may believe."

*I was regretting the past*
   *and fearing the future.*
*Suddenly God was speaking:*
   *"MY NAME IS 'I AM'"*
*I waited. God continued:*
   *"When you live in the past,*
   *with its mistakes and regrets,*
   *it is hard. I am not there.*
     *MY NAME IS NOT 'I WAS.'*
   *"When you live in the future,*
   *with its problems and fears,*
   *it is hard. I am not there.*
     *MY NAME IS NOT 'I WILL BE.'*
   *"When you live in this moment,*
   *it is not hard. I am here.*
     *MY NAME IS 'I AM.'"*

**Plaque on the wall of the ranch guesthouse kitchen**
St. Benedict's Monastery, Snowmass, Colorado

# I Am throughout John

| | |
|---|---|
| 1:19-23 | John the Baptizer's three "I Am Nots" |
| 4:26 | I Am |
| 6:20 | I Am |
| 6:35,41,48 | I am the bread of life |
| 8:12 | I am the light of the world |
| 8:24,28,58 | I Am |
| 9:5 | I am the light of the world |
| 10:7,9 | I am the sheep gate |
| 10:11,14 | I am the good shepherd |
| 11:25 | I am the resurrection and the life |
| 13:19 | I Am |
| 14:6 | I am the way, the truth, and the life |
| 15:1 | I am the true vine |
| 18:5-8 | I Am |
| 18:13-15;25-27 | Peter's three I Am Nots! |

# Assignment

Read the entire book of *John* with an eye for "I Am." Notice how *John* uses this thread skillfully throughout.

# Questions

How does *John* make the connection between Jesus, the man, and God who is known as Yahweh?

What strikes you about the I Am sayings?

What is your favorite I Am saying? Why?

What questions do you have?


Are John the Baptizer's "I'm nots" similar to Peter's?

# CHAPTER FIVE
# Signs of the Times

I grew up in Chattanooga, the home of Rock City. Wherever we traveled, we always knew how far we were from home because there were always signs, painted barns, and birdhouses that said, "See Rock City." My grandfather once journeyed all the way to Tokyo, Japan, where he saw a sign pointing east that said, "See Rock City – 6,768 Miles."

*John* talks of signs that Jesus performed. A sign points to something, somewhere, or someone. No one travels a distance to see a sign. They travel to see to whom or what the sign is pointing.

After the introductory poem centering on the Word (John 1:1-18), *John* uses narrative for the rest of the book. Some commentaries label the next section of the work (1:19 to 12:50) as "The Book of Signs."

In this section, seven signs are described by *John*. The author is careful to refer to these amazing acts of healing and wonder as "signs" (the Greek is *semeia)*. The Synoptics refer to these works of Jesus as "miracles" (the Greek is *dynamis* from which we derive words like "dynamite," "dynamic," and "dynamo").

*John* is all about Jesus' identity. The author relates the story of the signs so that those who came later could see what happened—what Jesus did. The teller recounts the signs which point to Jesus' identity during encounters with disease and natural forces.

Near the end of the book, *John* writes, "Then Jesus did many other signs in his disciples' presence, signs that aren't recorded in this scroll. But these things are written so that you will believe that Jesus is the Christ, God's Son, and that believing, you will have life in his name. (John 20:30-31, CEB).

*John* tells the reader/listener that the purpose of the signs is so you will believe that Jesus is the Christ, God's son, and that you will have life. These miraculous signs are important in *John* because they indicate that Jesus is the Messiah and connect to the words of the "coming one" found in Isaiah.

> *Make the minds of this people dull. Make their ears deaf and their eyes blind, so they can't see with their eyes or hear with their ears, or understand with their minds, and turn, and be healed.*
>
> **Isaiah 6:10, CEB**

> *On that day: The deaf will hear the words of a scroll and, freed from dimness and darkness, the eyes of the blind will see.*
>
> **Isaiah 29:18 (CEB)**

> *Then the eyes of those who can see will no longer be blind, the ears of those who can hear will listen*
>
> **Isaiah 32:3 (CEB)**

*Then the eyes of the blind will be opened,*
*and the ears of the deaf will be cleared.*

*Then the lame will leap like the deer,*
*and the tongue of the speechless will sing.*

*Waters will spring up in the desert,*
*and streams in the wilderness.*

**Isaiah 35:5-6 (CEB)**

*Hear, deaf ones, and blind ones, look and see.*

**Isaiah 42:18 (CEB)**

Luke tells this same story in a slightly different way. *John* places the signs throughout the book. Then at the end, he tells you why he did it: so that the reader would believe. Luke has John the Baptizer ask, "Are you the One?" Jesus responds by saying, "Tell him what you have seen and heard."

*When they reached Jesus, they said, "John the Baptist sent us to you. He asks, 'Are you the one who is coming, or should we look for someone else?'" Right then, Jesus healed many of their diseases, illnesses, and evil spirits, and he gave sight to a number of blind people. Then he replied to John's disciples, "Go, report to John what you have seen and heard. Those who were blind are able to see. Those who were crippled now walk. People with skin diseases are cleansed. Those who were deaf now hear. Those who were dead are raised up. And good news is preached to the poor. Happy is anyone who doesn't stumble along the way because of me."*

**Luke 7:20-23 (CEB)**

Every Christmas when our children and grandchildren gather at our house, we begin our celebration of Jesus' birth with a treasure hunt. Slender slips of paper hold clues. Each clue directs the children to the next clue until they find the treasure. It is a fun tradition. One year, the "treasure" was the news that a new family member would be arriving in July.

N.T. Wright wrote that the signs in *John* were clues to the treasure that is Jesus. The clues (signs) point to Jesus' identity and glory, but the clues are not the treasure itself. No one would confuse a clue with the treasure and simply stop the hunt. The clues lead one to a belief in Jesus[13]. People come to believe due to the signs or clues that Jesus left—breadcrumbs in the wilderness, if you will, that lead to Jesus himself in his full identity as the Word in flesh.

"The issue is not whether people profess belief in signs but whether they exhibit their belief [in Jesus] by their lives."[14]

The purpose of the signs is to elicit belief. *John* attempts to report the signs to those who were not there. In a sense, *John* is helping the hearer—us—see the signs more clearly. The storytelling style brings the hearer into the action, which is storytelling at its best.

- Jesus challenged a certain royal official: "Unless you see miraculous signs and wonders you won't believe." (4:48).

---

13 N.T. Wright, *John for Everyone, Part One, p. 20,* Westminster John Knox Press, 2004.

14 Dennis E. Smith, *Storyteller's Companion to the Bible, John, Volume Ten,* Abingdon Press, p. 17, 1996.

- During the healing of the lame man at the pool of Siloam, Jesus said, "These works I do testify about me that the Father sent me." (5:36).
- During the Festival of Dedication, Jesus addressed the Jewish opposition: "If I don't do the works of my Father, don't believe me. But if I do them, and you don't believe me, believe the works so that you can know and recognize that the Father is in me and I am in the Father." (10:37-38).

# Signs in John's Story

### The First Sign – Wedding Wine (John 2:1-11)

*Jesus replied, "Woman, what does that have to do with me? My time hasn't come yet."*

*His mother told the servants, "Do whatever he tells you." Nearby were six stone water jars used for the Jewish cleansing ritual, each able to hold about twenty or thirty gallons.*

*Jesus said to the servants, "Fill the jars with water," and they filled them to the brim. Then he told them, "Now draw some from them and take it to the headwaiter," and they did. The headwaiter tasted the water that had become wine. He didn't know where it came from, though the servants who had drawn the water knew.*

**John 2:4-9 (CEB)**

### A Few Observations on this Story

#### *First appearance of Jesus' mother*

*John* never uses the name "Mary" to refer to Jesus' mother in his book. Notice that Jesus' mother does not tell Jesus what to do. She simply informs him they have run out of wine. She does tell the servants to do whatever Jesus tells them to do.

### *Time (Timing)*

This is the first mention of "My time," the first of many mentions!

### *Ritual Cleansing*

Six large stone jars to keep people ritually clean. Six is significant since it denotes almost-but-not-quite-perfect since seven is the number of perfection. The rites are significant but not quite enough.

### *Large Amount of Water (Wine)*

The jars held between 20 and 30 gallons each, or 120 to 180 gallons collectively. In a place and time when water was carried, this was an excessive amount. This amount of water required a lot of work to bring from a well.

### *Reverse Order*

The best wine is served last. The steward (and the audience) knew this was the wrong order. You always serve the best first; then, when people get a little tipsy and are not as discerning, you serve the less good wine. In other places, Jesus talks about life in the kingdom as being in the reverse order: the first shall be last and the last shall be first. The best wine is a sign of the kingdom.

### *Credentials*

Clarence Jordan in the *Cotton Patch Version of John* translates the phrase "He revealed his glory" as "he showed his credentials," simply meaning, this was a sign pointing to Jesus' glory, and thus, his identity.

## Eucharist

The first sign in *John* points to Jesus who offered wine at a wedding feast—wonderful symbols of the Kingdom. *John* does not relate the institution of the Lord's Supper as the Synoptics do. However, the Eucharist pervades the entire book. Look for other references in *John* to the Eucharist/Communion.

## An Interesting Thought

In Jordan's translation, he offers this footnote on the wedding wine:

> *The Greek word here means to draw water from a well with a bucket. The same word is used in John 4:7: "A woman from Samaria came to draw (or bucket up) water." Obviously, then, the servants got the water for the emcee from the same source as they got water to fill the jars—from the well. The well turned to wine, not the water in the stone jars (the Mosaic laws), now supplies the good wine which delights the emcee. This first "sign" perhaps points to the fact that the same God (the well) who gave the law on Sinai, now fulfills it by giving grace (the wine as a symbol of shed blood) on Calvary. Men taste of law and say, "It's good," but they taste of grace and say, "You've saved the best till last."*
>
> **Clarence Jordan**
> *The Cotton Patch Version of Matthew and John*, p. 105

## The Second Sign – Long Distance Sign (John 4:46-54)

*When he heard that Jesus was coming from Judea to Galilee, he went out to meet him and asked Jesus if he would come and heal his son, for his son was about to die. Jesus said to him, "Unless you see miraculous signs and wonders, you won't believe."*

*The royal official said to him, "Lord, come before my son dies."*

*Jesus replied, "Go home. Your son lives." The man believed the word that Jesus spoke to him and set out for his home.*

**John 4:47-50 (CEB)**

## A Few Observations on this Story

### *Location (Cana)*

This second sign occurs near the first one—Cana in Galilee—which ties the two signs together. In the first sign, Jesus' mother tells him there is no wine, and Jesus responds by saying, "My hour has not come." Yet, he still performs the sign. In this one, the royal official asks Jesus to come and heal his son, and Jesus responds with some feeling about people just wanting to see signs. Jesus again performs the sign but not the way requested. The man asks Jesus to come with him, and Jesus does not go.

### *Synoptics*

This is one of the few stories in *John* that is found in other gospels (Matthew 8:5-13 and Luke 7:1-10).

### Royal Official

This could be any type of official. He could have been one of Herod's people or one of the Roman emperor's people. He also could have been a Gentile, but that is not the point of this particular episode.

### Hour

In the first sign, Jesus said it is not time. In this one, the "hour," or the time, is significant to the royal official. The timing of Jesus' words with the healing causes the royal official and his entire household to believe.

### The Word

The royal official believed the word of Jesus. When he heard Jesus speak, he left to go home. Jesus said, "Unless you see miraculous signs and wonders, you won't believe" (Look at John 20:29). This person believes long before he sees. He comes to believe simply from Jesus speaking. Jesus rejects a trust that is built only from witnessing miracles in one's own life. Also, when Jesus speaks the word, wondrous events occur—just as when God spoke, and creation occurred.

## The Third Sign - Healing at the Pool (John 5:1-47)

> *A certain man was there who had been sick for thirty-eight years. When Jesus saw him lying there, knowing that he had already been there a long time, he asked him, "Do you want to get well?"*
>
> *The sick man answered him, "Sir, I don't have anyone who can put me in the water when it is stirred up. When I'm*

*trying to get to it, someone else has gotten in ahead of me."*

*Jesus said to him, "Get up! Pick up your mat and walk." Immediately the man was well, and he picked up his mat and walked. Now that day was the Sabbath.*

*The Jewish leaders said to the man who had been healed, "It's the Sabbath; you aren't allowed to carry your mat."*

*He answered, "The man who made me well said to me, 'Pick up your mat and walk.'"*

*They inquired, "Who is this man who said to you, 'Pick it up and walk'?" The man who had been cured didn't know who it was, because Jesus had slipped away from the crowd gathered there.*

**John 5:5-12 (CEB)**

## A Few Observations on this Story

### *Verse 4*

In most modern translations, the end of verse 3 and verse 4 are left out. The manuscript evidence shows that these verses were probably added later as an explanation of why the waters of Siloam were "stirred" or "troubled."

### *Initiative*

Jesus takes the initiative. Unlike the two previous signs, Jesus is not asked to do something. Instead, he asks the crippled man, "Do you want to be healed?" An interesting question to one who had been hanging around a healing spot for thirty-eight years!

### *Unknown Healer*

The man doesn't even know who healed him. *John* also does not give this man's name. We only know it is a man who is lame and cannot get healed due to his condition. The man clings to hope for healing. After all, he has hung around for thirty-eight years.

### *Sabbath*

Jesus is often challenged about "working" on the Sabbath. Jesus uses this sign to point to the new day when God will heal. Jesus points to The Sabbath, the Day of God.

### *Conversations*

This sign provokes much discussion. The healed man, Jesus, and the Jewish authorities all have parts in talking about the Sabbath and testimony.

### *Time*

In verse 25, Jesus says, "The time is coming—and is here!—when the dead will hear the voice of God's Son, and those who hear it will live." "Time" is mentioned again in connection to a sign. The time to listen is now!

## The Fourth Sign - Eating in the Wilderness (John 6:1-15)

> *Jesus looked up and saw the large crowd coming toward him. He asked Philip, "Where will we buy food to feed these people?" Jesus said this to test him, for he already knew what he was going to do.*
>
> *Philip replied, "More than a half year's salary worth of food wouldn't be enough for each person to have even a little bit."*
>
> *One of his disciples, Andrew, Simon Peter's brother, said, "A youth here has five barley loaves and two fish. But what good is that for a crowd like this?"*

*Jesus said, "Have the people sit down." There was plenty of grass there. They sat down, about five thousand of them. Then Jesus took the bread. When he had given thanks, he distributed it to those who were sitting there. He did the same with the fish, each getting as much as they wanted.*

**John 6:5-11 (CEB)**

## A Few Observations on this Story

### *The Synoptics*

This is the only miracle/sign story that the four gospels share (Matthew 14:13-21, Mark 6:30-44, and Luke 9:10-17).

### *Common elements between the four gospels:*

- Five loaves and two fish. *John* tells of another meal of fish and bread at the very end of the book in John 21. The original audience would have heard this connection.
- Five thousand men (implying the crowd was larger).
- Seated = recline, "Have the people sit down" is a poor translation. The actual words *anaklino* and *anapipto* mean to lie down or recline. A few English translations get this right. Modern translators are trying to capture the sense of the word. Think of da Vinci's painting *The Last Supper*. Da Vinci tried to reimagine the scene so that people of his day would understand it. No one today reclines to eat. However, this is one of the moments of poetry which a translation can miss or ruin.
- Grass – Luke is the only one who does not mention grass. Mark even calls it "green grass." *John* says Jesus had them lie down in the grass.

- "Blessed and broke" is part of the formula for the Eucharist, or Communion. The phrase is found in Matthew, Mark, Luke, and Paul's accounts of the Last Supper. *John* evokes the Eucharist even by adding that this wilderness feast took place near the Passover.
- All ate until satisfied. This was not a snack but a banquet in which all were filled. Another reference to God's excessive abundance.
- Leftovers. All four gospels show that Jesus supplied beyond everyone's hunger. A bounty of leftovers enough to feed all of Israel with twelve baskets.

### *Location*

"Across the Galilee Sea." Jesus and his students move from where the work with miraculous signs has been performed, but the crowd follows, looking for more signs. The mass of people left their homes and are now far from them.

### *Conversation*

Philip and Jesus talk, and then Andrew joins in the exchange. Only *John* identifies which students were involved in the conversation.

### *Sign*

The people see to whom the sign is pointing: "This is truly the prophet who is coming into the world."

### *Retreat*

Jesus leaves the group, not because of physical danger but because the crowd with the disciples presumably wants to make him king. The danger is being made king before it is time.

## The Fifth Sign – A Dark and Stormy Night
(John 6:16-21)

> *When evening came, Jesus' disciples went down to the lake. They got into a boat and were crossing the lake to Capernaum. It was already getting dark and Jesus hadn't come to them yet. The water was getting rough because a strong wind was blowing. When the wind had driven them out for about three or four miles, they saw Jesus walking on the water. He was approaching the boat and they were afraid. He said to them, "I Am. Don't be afraid." Then they wanted to take him into the boat, and just then the boat reached the land where they had been heading.*
>
> **John 6:16-21 (CEB)**

### A Few Observations on This Story

#### *Translation*

Again, the poetry of this moment is lost in some English translations. In verse 20, Jesus says, "I Am." He does not say, "It is I." Jesus uses God's name.

#### *Genesis 1:2*

"…the earth was without shape or form, it was dark over the deep sea, and God's wind swept over the waters" (Genesis 1:2). *John* describes the setting as being dark on rough waters due to the strong wind. He is referring to the Creator of the Universe, the Word (John 1:2-3).

### *Other accounts*

Matthew 14:22-33 (Peter's walk with Jesus on the water) and Mark 6:45-52. Both accounts also follow the feeding of the five thousand. Luke has a story of Jesus calming a storm (Luke 8), but it is different from this account in that Jesus is in the boat. That telling is recounted in Matthew 8 and Mark 4 as well, but it does not appear in *John*.

### *Calming the Storm*

In *John's* telling, Jesus does not calm the storm, he simply brings them safely to shore.

## The Sixth Sign – Only the Blind See (John 9:1-41)

> *As Jesus walked along, he saw a man who was blind from birth. Jesus' disciples asked, "Rabbi, who sinned so that he was born blind, this man or his parents?"*
>
> *Jesus answered, "Neither he nor his parents. This happened so that God's mighty works might be displayed in him. While it's daytime, we must do the works of him who sent me. Night is coming when no one can work. While I am in the world, I am the light of the world." After he said this, he spit on the ground, made mud with the saliva, and smeared the mud on the man's eyes. Jesus said to him, "Go, wash in the pool of Siloam" (this word means "sent"). So the man went away and washed. When he returned, he could see.*
>
> **John 9:1-7 (CEB)**

## A Few Observations on this Story

Seriously? Even a blind man can see what this one is about!

### *Theological Discussion*

Upon encountering the blind man, the disciples want to have a theological discussion about the origins of the man's blindness. The Pharisees spend a lot of time trying to track down the meaning of what happened. They interviewed the man and his parents and ultimately decided the man was sinful (a theological conclusion).

### *Irony*

Only the blind man sees what is going on. Everyone else—even the disciples—is stumbling about trying to find answers.

### *Light and Dark*

The themes of light and dark move from discussion and poetry to real-life examples. To see requires light. To be in the dark is to be blind.

### *The Healed Man*

Represents a person of faith. One who met Jesus and could see who Jesus really is. He is also very practical. "Where is he?" they ask. "I don't know! All I know is that I was blind and now I see." An interesting commentary on how people experience the love of God in Jesus. The man experienced Jesus. Everyone else wants to talk about what his experience was and what it meant.

### *Banishment from the Synagogue*

The man is threatened with banishment from the

synagogue (9:22). Many commentaries postulate that this banishment was similar to the original congregations hearing the story. The first Christians were Jews who saw Jesus as the fulfillment of the Law.

### *Invisible Jesus*

As he did after healing of the man by the pool, Jesus just blends into the crowd. Jesus performs this wondrous sign and then is not seen. Again, the original hearers of this story would have "seen" this fact of Jesus at work invisibly as their own experience of him. Think about it. Even the blind man did not see Jesus perform this sign. He only saw the result of what Jesus did.

### *The Parents*

I like the fact that the parents did not want to get in the middle of this fight. "Ask him yourself. He's old enough to answer for himself."

## The Seventh Sign – A Resurrection (John 11:1-48)

> *Martha said to Jesus, "Lord, if you had been here, my brother wouldn't have died. Even now I know that whatever you ask God, God will give you."*
>
> *Jesus told her, "Your brother will rise again."*
>
> *Martha replied, "I know that he will rise in the resurrection on the last day."*
>
> *Jesus said to her, "I am the resurrection and the life. Whoever believes in me will live, even though they die. Everyone who lives and believes in me will never die. Do you believe this?"*
>
> *She replied, "Yes, Lord, I believe that you are the Christ, God's Son, the one who is coming into the world."*

*After she said this, she went and spoke privately to her sister Mary, "The teacher is here and he's calling for you." When Mary heard this, she got up quickly and went to Jesus. He hadn't entered the village but was still in the place where Martha had met him. When the Jews who were comforting Mary in the house saw her get up quickly and leave, they followed her. They assumed she was going to mourn at the tomb.*

*When Mary arrived where Jesus was and saw him, she fell at his feet and said, "Lord, if you had been here, my brother wouldn't have died."*

*When Jesus saw her crying and the Jews who had come with her crying also, he was deeply disturbed and troubled. He asked, "Where have you laid him?"*

*They replied, "Lord, come and see."*

*Jesus began to cry. The Jews said, "See how much he loved him!" But some of them said, "He healed the eyes of the man born blind. Couldn't he have kept Lazarus from dying?"*

*Jesus was deeply disturbed again when he came to the tomb. It was a cave, and a stone covered the entrance. Jesus said, "Remove the stone."*

*Martha, the sister of the dead man, said, "Lord, the smell will be awful! He's been dead four days."*

*Jesus replied, "Didn't I tell you that if you believe, you will see God's glory?" So they removed the stone. Jesus looked up and said, "Father, thank you for hearing me. I know you always hear me. I say this for the benefit of the crowd standing here so that they will believe that you sent me." Having said this, Jesus shouted with a loud voice, "Lazarus, come out!" The dead man came out, his feet bound and his hands tied, and his face covered with a cloth. Jesus said to them, "Untie him and let him go."*

*Therefore, many of the Jews who came with Mary and saw what Jesus did believed in him.*

**John 11:21-45 (CEB)**

## A Few Observations on this Story

### *Time*

"Twelve hours" in verse 9. Also, timing: almost like the wedding feast. Jesus does things on his own time. Jesus delays going to Bethany. Jesus is working on a different timetable, as he told his mother at the wedding in Cana.

### *Bethany*

House of the poor.

### *Another Theological Discussion*

Jesus told Martha, "Your brother will rise again." You can almost hear Martha sigh. "Yes, yes, I know he will rise in the last days." Jesus moves her away from a belief in the resurrection to himself. "I am the resurrection and the life."

### *Statement of Identity*

Similar to Peter's at John 6:68-69. *John* puts this affirmation into Martha's mouth. This type of statement of faith occurs multiple times in *John*. John the Baptizer (1:15;29), Andrew (1:41), Philip (1:45), Nathanael (1:49), Peter (6:68-69), Mary Magdalene (20:18), Thomas (20:28), the Beloved Disciple (21:7), and the author (20:30). The proclamation of Jesus as the One, the Messiah, the Christ, Lord and God, and simply the Lord permeates *John's* telling of Jesus' life. The listener hears it over and over from many mouths.

### Shortest verse

"Jesus wept" (11:35). As children, we loved this verse because we could quote the Bible from memory. The writer conveys in a short sentence the love and compassion of Jesus. This passage shows the power of Patterson's Language I. It takes very few words to carry a sense of Jesus' heart.

### Mary and Martha

Martha and Mary appear in Luke 10:38-42. There is no mention of Lazarus or Bethany in Luke's account. It is probably best to focus on the way *John* tells the story instead of bringing in Luke's version. This account is the only time the two women are mentioned in *John*. The author does refer to Mary as the one who anointed Jesus with perfume and with her hair (11:2) and then tells that story immediately after Lazarus' resurrection (12:11).

### The Significance of Being the Seventh Sign

The fact that the number of signs is seven is no accident. The author likes numerical symbols (Look at six large jars in 2:1-11, six days in 12:1, and twelve baskets of leftovers in 6:13, among many others). This last sign points to Jesus' own resurrection. In this story, Jesus says, "I am the resurrection and the life" (11:25).

## The Eighth Sign – THE Ultimate Sign (John 20-21)

In the section referred to as the "Book of Signs" (John 1:19–John 12:50), there are seven signs. However, there is actually an eighth sign, but some people do not count it because it happens to Jesus instead of Jesus performing the work himself. This eighth, and last, sign is beyond perfection. It is the ultimate sign of who Jesus is as the Son of the Living God. We hear Jesus' identity proclaimed throughout these final pages of *John's* account.

Note that this eighth sign occurs on the eighth day—not on the Sabbath when God rests as Jesus rests in the tomb but on the first day of the week, the first day of the new creation when God begins anew in the Risen Jesus.

### *Miraculous Catch of Fish – (21:1-11)*

One could argue that this story reveals yet another sign, throwing off the numerology of *John*. Many argue the story was added later. True or not, it is a sign of the resurrection of the Lord and a wonderful story either way. (See "Breakfast on the Beach," p. 183).

---

*John* does not spend time explaining the signs. *John* shares them in a way that the audience can see the sign and thus, in seeing, can believe. The wonderful allusions are often subtle (i.e., Psalm 23 at the feeding of the five thousand; the Eucharist at the wedding feast and feeding of the five thousand; Jesus' people coming through the waters to safety as he walked on the sea; the chaotic waters of creation amid darkness and wind echo the first sentences of Genesis; etc.

*John* is telling the story of Jesus. He uses the works of Jesus—particularly the "signs"—to show who Jesus is. To examine the signs too closely is to miss the point.

*John* is not about the signs themselves, but about the one to whom the signs point. The story of the wedding wine is not about the wine but about the one who is the wine. The story about feeding the five thousand is about the good shepherd who is the "bread of heaven." Lazarus' death and resurrection is about the one who is "the resurrection and the life."

> *This man is doing many miraculous signs! If we let him go on like this, everyone will believe in him. Then the Romans will come and take away both our temple and our people.*
> **John 11:48 (CEB)**

> *The crowd who had been with him when he called Lazarus out of the tomb and raised him from the dead were testifying about him. That's why the crowd came to meet him, because they had heard about this miraculous sign that he had done. Therefore, the Pharisees said to each other, "See! You've accomplished nothing! Look! The whole world is following him!"*
> **John 12:17-19 (CEB)**

## Signs in the *Gospel of John*

| | |
|---|---|
| Wedding Wine | 2:1-11 |
| Long Distance Sign | 4:46b-54 |
| Healing at the Pool | 5:2-47 |
| Eating in the Wilderness | 6:1-15 |
| A Dark and Stormy Night | 6:16-21 |
| Only The Blind See | 9:1-41 |
| A Resurrection | 11:1-44 |
| The Ultimate Sign | 20-21 |

# Assignment

Reread the entire *Gospel of John*. Try a different translation. Make note of the "clues to the treasure."

# Questions

Did you notice anything you had not seen before?

What is the difference between a "sign" and a "miracle"?

Which "sign" episode in *John* is your favorite? Why?

Did Jesus perform all the miraculous signs in the same manner?

As you read through the "sign" episodes where did you find yourself? An observer? A disciple? The one being healed, fed, resurrected? Other?

Where did you see other signs or allusions to the Eucharist/Communion/Lord's Supper?

## CHAPTER SIX
# He Pitched a Tent, Glory Be!

*Pulpiteers will censure*
*Our instinctive venture*
*Into what they call*
*The material*
*When we took that fall*
*From the apple tree.*
*But God's own descent*
*Into flesh was meant*
*As a demonstration*
*That the supreme merit*
*Lay in risking spirit*
*In substantiation.*

*Spirit enters flesh*
*And for all it's worth*
*Charges into earth*
*In birth after birth*
*Ever fresh and fresh.*
*We may take the view*
*That its derring-do*
*Thought of in the large*
*Was one mighty charge*
*On our human part*
*Of the soul's ethereal*
*Into the material.*

**From Robert Frost's Kitty Hawk**

*Though he was in the form of God,*
 *he did not consider being equal with God something to exploit.*

*But he emptied himself*
 *by taking the form of a slave*
 *and by becoming like human beings.*
 *When he found himself in the form of a human,*

*he humbled himself by becoming obedient to the point of death, even death on a cross.*

*Therefore, God highly honored him*
 *and gave him a name above all names,*

*so that at the name of Jesus everyone*
 *in heaven, on earth, and under the earth might bow*

*and every tongue confess*
 *that Jesus Christ is Lord, to the glory of God the Father.*

**Philippians 2:6-11 (CEB)**

*Therefore, the Lord will give you a sign. The young woman is pregnant and is about to give birth to a son, and she will name him Immanuel [God is with us].*

**Isaiah 7:14 (CEB)**

*It will rise up over all its channels, overflowing all its banks, and sweep into Judah, flooding, overflowing, and reaching up to the neck. But God is with us [Immanuel]; the span of his wings will cover the width of the land.*

**Isaiah 8:7b-8 (CEB)**

*The Word become flesh. Ultimate Mystery born with a skull you could crush one-handed. Incarnation. It is not tame. It is not touching. It is not beautiful. It is uninhabitable terror. It is unthinkable darkness riven with unbearable light. Agonized laboring led to it, vast upheavals of intergalactic space/time split apart, a wrenching and tearing of the very sineuws of reality itself. You can only cover your eyes and shudder before it, before this: "God of God, Light of Light, very God of very God . . . who for us and for our salvation," as the Nicene Creed puts it, "came down from heaven."*

*"Came down. Only then do we dare uncover our eyes and see what we can see. It is the Resurrection and the Life she holds in her arms. It is the bitterness of death he takes at her breast."*

**Frederick Buechner**
Whistling in the Dark – A Doubter's Dictionary

The entire book of *John* is summarized in one verse:

*The Word became flesh
and made his home among us.
We have seen his glory,
glory like that of a father's only son,
full of grace and truth.*

**John 1:14 (CEB)**

The Word that created the universe came "risking spirit in substantiation" (Frost). The Apostle Paul quoted a poem in his letter to the church at Philippi saying that God emptied himself and became human, humbling himself to live a human life and to die a human death.

*John* begins with Genesis 1:1, "In the beginning." He then draws on Genesis 1:26 where the text reports that God created humans in God's own likeness, in God's image. However, in 1:14, *John* reverses the formula of Genesis 1:26. God comes in human likeness. A human made in the image of God is turned on its head, and *John* presents Jesus as God in human likeness. This is scandalous!

*John* intentionally and carefully uses the word "to pitch a tent" or "to tabernacle" in (1:14) where it is often translated "dwell." The thread of the tabernacle (Tent of Meeting), or the temple (a more substantial substitute for the tabernacle), runs throughout *John's* narrative. Spliced onto the tabernacle thread is the thread of glory. These two themes are intertwined for the whole narrative.

As the children of Israel followed Moses from Egyptian slavery to God's Promised Land, they crossed a wilderness area. God saved them from Pharoah's army, fed them manna and quail, slaked their thirst with the waters of Meribah. One response to God's bounty was to build a tent (or tabernacle) in which to meet with God. Some translations call it the "Tent of Meeting" or the "Meeting Tent."

The tabernacle represented the place where God and humans met. Moses and Aaron took thank offerings to God in the tabernacle. They also conferred with the Lord in this tent which was carefully and wonderfully made.

> *They should make me a sanctuary so I can be present among them.*
> **Exodus 25:8 (CEB)**

> *I will place my dwelling among you, and I will not despise you. I will walk around among you; I will be your God, and you will be my people.*
> **Leviticus 26:11-12 (CEB)**

Again, remember that *John* draws on this one verse (1:14) throughout his telling of Jesus' life. The Word became flesh in the tabernacle that is Jesus. But *John* goes on to say, "We have seen his glory, glory like that of a father's only son, full of grace and truth," meaning when one sees Jesus, they see and experience the glory of God.

> *When Moses had finished all the work, the cloud covered the meeting tent and the Lord's glorious presence filled the dwelling. Moses couldn't enter the meeting tent because the cloud had settled on it, and the Lord's glorious presence filled the dwelling.*
>
> **Exodus 40:33b-35 (CEB)**

> *Aaron then raised his hands toward the people and blessed them. After performing the purification offering, the entirely burned offering, and the well-being sacrifice, he came down. Moses and Aaron then entered the meeting tent. When they came out, they blessed the people, and the Lord's glorious presence appeared to all the people.*
>
> **Leviticus 9:22-23 (CEB)**

*John* spends the rest of the book emphasizing the incarnation and the glorious presence of God in Jesus. *John* wastes no time. Immediately after the poetic prologue of 1:1-18, John the Baptizer points to Jesus and proclaims, "Look! There is the Lamb of God." The very terminology, "the Lamb of God," evokes images of the temple. Lambs were sacrificed in the temple. In John the Baptizer's words lies the climax of the story: the cross.

In addition to the temple image of the Lamb of God, the picture of the lamb also evokes the lamb supplied by God when Abraham was about to sacrifice his own son. The lamb is a rich image bearing many layers of meaning.

Only a few sentences later, Andrew tells his brother, Simon, "We have found the Messiah," which is translated "Christ" (1:41). Next, Philip tells his friend, Nathanael, "We have found the one Moses wrote about in the Law and the Prophets: Jesus, Joseph's son, from Nazareth." (1:45) Then Nathanael declares, "Rabbi, you are God's Son. You are the king of Israel" (1:49).

Do you see *John's* artistry? Do you see how in only a few sentences of conversation *John* proclaims over and over who Jesus is and what he will do.

Next, Jesus himself alludes to Jacob's ladder (Genesis 28:1-15) where Jacob receives the promise of God's protection and a future. Jesus says, "You will see heaven open and God's angels going up to heaven and down to earth on the Human One" (1:51). Jesus is the ladder connecting earth and heaven. Jesus is also the Tent of Meeting where humans and God meet.

These first paragraphs reveal many aspects of Jesus. The disciples (and the original audience as well as modern readers) are invited to "Come and See."

*John* locates much of the story in or near the temple in Jerusalem—with the temple that is Jesus. *John* makes sure you will not miss the point by relating the story of Jesus in the temple. Jesus demands cleansing: "Get these things out of here! Don't make my Father's house a place of business." *John* then quotes Psalm 69:9 so you won't miss the point: "Passion for your house consumes me."

Jesus says of himself, "Destroy this temple and in

three days I'll raise it up." The Jewish leaders don't get what he is saying, but *John's* audience did!

Much later in the book, Jesus is back at the temple, and the Jewish leaders are once more doubting who Jesus actually is. They say:

> *We know where he is from, but when the Christ comes, no one will know where he is from.*
>
> *While Jesus was teaching in the temple, he exclaimed, "You know me and where I am from. I haven't come on my own. The one who sent me is true, and you don't know him. I know him because I am from him and he sent me.*
>
> **John 7:27-29 (CEB)**

In addition to Jesus being the temple, God's glory is located in him as God's glory was in the actual temple. The theme of glory permeates the *Gospel of John*. The word "glory" *(doxa)* holds many meanings:

- Splendor, brightness (such as the moon, sun, and stars)
- Grace, magnificence, dignity
- An aspect belonging to God
- Majesty, like that of a king
- The condition of blessedness promised to true followers of Jesus

The noun "glory" and the verb "glorify" appear many times throughout the book. The idea of glory is a bright thread that weaves in and out of many episodes. Below are only a few examples of this word "glory."

## Glory

- 1:14 – "The Word became flesh and made his home among us. We have seen his **glory**, **glory** like that of a father's only son, full of grace and truth."
- 2:11 – "This was the first miraculous sign that Jesus did in Cana of Galilee. He revealed his **glory**, and his disciples believed in him."
- 7:18 – "Those who speak on their own seek **glory** for themselves. Those who seek the **glory** of him who sent me are people of truth; there's no falsehood in them."
- 8:50 – "I'm not trying to bring **glory** to myself. There's one who is seeking to **glorify** me, and he's the judge."
- 8:54 – "Jesus answered, 'If I **glorify** myself, my **glory** is meaningless. My Father, who you say is your God, is the one who glorifies me.'"
- 11:4 – "When he heard this, Jesus said, 'This illness isn't fatal. It's for the **glory** of God so that God's Son can be **glorified** through it.'"
- 11:40 – "Jesus replied, 'Didn't I tell you that if you believe, you will see God's **glory**?'"
- 12:28 – "'Father, **glorify** your name!' Then a voice came from heaven, 'I have **glorified** it, and I will **glorify** it again.'"
- 13:32 – "If God has been **glorified** in him, God will also **glorify** the Human One in himself and will **glorify** him immediately."

- 17:1 – "When Jesus finished saying these things, he looked up to heaven and said, 'Father, the time has come. **Glorify** your Son, so that the Son can **glorify** you.'"

The Jewish leaders try to trap Jesus, to eliminate him, to nail him down. In contemporary culture, there is often a move to entrap God on the pages of the Bible. Some desire to codify Jesus' life in such a way that he is confined to ink and paper. Our natural human tendency is to want laws, a set of rules that can be followed. We do best when we can check things off a list. We remain in control. We feel safer. We, like the Jewish leaders in *John*, feel closer to God by keeping the rules.

As Jesus tells Nicodemus, God is wind/spirit/breath. God moves where God will. You can't really nail God down. Jesus invites people to come and see what God is doing. Jesus says, "If you want to see God, then watch me." *John* works to make Jesus visible so that others can see God. One way *John* does this is with references to "time." The clock ticks during the whole book. (I am aware there were no ticking clocks in *John's* day, but you get the point. Perhaps the image is that of the shadow on the sundial progressing toward the end of the day.)

The following are references to time:

## What Time Is It? Chart

| Verse | Reference |
|---|---|
| 1:39 | Four p.m. |
| 2:4 | Not my time—not yet. |
| 4:21 | The time is coming. |
| 4:23 | The time is coming—and is here! |
| 4:35 | Time for the harvest—ripe for the harvest. |
| 4:52 | What time did my son get well? About one p.m. |
| 5:25 | The time is coming—and is here! |
| 5:28 | The time is coming. |
| 7:6 | My time hasn't come yet. |
| 7:8 | My time hasn't come yet. |
| 7:30 | His time hadn't come yet. |
| 8:20 | His time hadn't come yet. |
| 12:23 | The time has come for the Human One to be glorified. |
| 12:27 | And what shall I say, "Father, save me from this time?" No, for this is the reason I have come to this time. |
| 12:31 | Now is the time for the judgment of this world. |
| 13:1 | Jesus knew that his time had come to leave this world and go to the Father. |
| 16:2 | The time is coming when those who kill you will think that they are doing a service to God. |
| 16:21 | She has pain because her time has come. |
| 16:25 | The time is coming when I will no longer speak to you in such analogies. |
| 16:32 | Look! A time is coming—and is here!—when each of you will be scattered. |
| 17:1 | He looked up to heaven and said, "Father, the time has come. Glorify your Son, so that the Son can glorify you. |
| 19:20 | It is completed. (It is finished. It is fulfilled. It is achieved.) |

The climax of the story of Jesus comes with Jesus' own words: "It is completed!" Remember, last words in a story are very important. Jesus' final words are, "We are done! It is fulfilled. It is all achieved. It is finished."

*John* has more to tell before he is through with Jesus' story, but the climax to which he has been writing is in Jesus' last words from the cross. Heaven and earth meet. God's glory shines in Jesus. It has all come together in this time.

The resurrection stories—on the first day of the week, in the locked room, on the beach—all show Jesus present with those who live after the crucifixion. The Resurrection occurs not on the Sabbath or the Passover but on the first day of the week. God rests on the Sabbath while Jesus is in the tomb. Creation begins anew on the first day of the week. Again, *John* uses "time" skillfully to communicate the greater theme of the new creation. *John* begins the story in 1:1 with the creation, and he ends with the new creation when the old has passed away and new life is available, hence that last story about Simon Peter's forgiveness.

*John* tells Jesus' story in such a manner that future disciples can "see" him. The narrative connects the listener with the Living Jesus and invites everyone and anyone to "come and see."

# Assignment

Read through the entire *Gospel of John* one more time. Look for references and allusions to the temple and sacrifice. Underline, or mark, the times that glory and glorify are mentioned. See how often *John* mentions time.

# Questions

What struck you in this sixth reading of the *Gospel of John*? Did you see something you had missed?

What other references to time, the time of day, or the time of the month did you see?

What is your favorite part of *John's* telling of Jesus' story? Why?

Were you able to see the themes of Incarnation, glory, and time? Could you see Jesus more clearly?

How have you come to see Jesus? Have you seen him in new ways? What are they?

Did you notice that nearly half of the book is the story of the last week of Jesus' life? Why would *John* give that one week so much space?

# Epilogue

*Then Jesus did many other miraculous signs in his disciples' presence, signs that aren't recorded in this scroll. But these things are written so that you will believe that Jesus is the Christ, God's Son, and that believing, you will have life in his name.*

**John 20:30-31 CEB**

The legendary Marco Polo left his hometown of Venice at seventeen with his father and uncle. The Polos trekked across the trade routes to China, met the mighty Kublai Khan, traveled throughout China and Southeast Asia, and lived in Asia for twenty-four years. After their return home, Marco Polo, then forty-one, fought in a sea battle during which he was captured. He spent time in prison. He dictated tales of his adventures and his years in Asia from his prison cell.

His book—*The Travels of Marco Polo*—spread throughout Europe. Polo's stories about the incredible advances of China's culture and people amused some and stunned others. Many called Polo's book a pack of lies, pure fabrication. The book was banned in some places.

The story goes that when Marco Polo was dying, his family summoned a priest. Polo confessed his sins. The priest hesitated to administer the last rites. When Polo asked, "Why do you wait?" The priest replied, "You must confess ALL your sins."

"I have done so to the best of my memory."

"What about the sinful lies you have told?"

To which Marco Polo replied, "I haven't told the half of it."

It is not possible to tell everything about the *Gospel of John*. The book is too complex while at the same time so wonderfully simple. This study is meant to assist you in seeing *John's* art and artistry in storytelling. *John* wanted you to see and believe in Jesus.

Many good commentaries are listed in the resources. Draw on those resources, but first and foremost, READ *John*. More than once or even twice...

> *Jesus did many other things as well. If all of them were recorded, I imagine the world itself wouldn't have enough room for the scrolls that would be written.*
>
> **John 21:25**

# MEDITATIONS
## on John's Gospel

# Words and the Word

*In the beginning was the Word*
  *and the Word was with God*
  *and the Word was God.*
*The Word was with God in the beginning.*
*Everything came into being through the Word,*
  *and without the Word*
  *nothing came into being.*
*What came into being*
  *through the Word was life,*
  *and the life was the light for all people.*
*The light shines in the darkness,*
  *and the darkness doesn't extinguish the light.*

*A man named John was sent from God. He came
as a witness to testify concerning the light, so that
through him everyone would believe in the light. He
himself wasn't the light, but his mission was to testify
concerning the light.*

*The true light that shines on all people*
  *was coming into the world.*
*The light was in the world,*
  *and the world came into being through the light,*
    *but the world didn't recognize the light.*
*The light came to his own people,*
  *and his own people didn't welcome him.*
*But those who did welcome him,*
    *those who believed in his name,*
  *he authorized to become God's children,*
    *born not from blood*
    *nor from human desire or passion,*
    *but born from God.*

*The Word became flesh*
  *and made his home among us.*
*We have seen his glory,*
  *glory like that of a father's only son,*
    *full of grace and truth.*

**John 1:1-14 (CEB)**

An old mountain story tells of a man who has been away from home for a long time. When he comes back to town, he runs into one of his old friends.

"Howdy, Zeke."

"Howdy."

"How ye be?"

"Fine as frog hair! How ye be?"

"No complaints. What's the news?"

"News? News? No news at all."

"Oh, Zeke. Surely something has happened. I been gone nigh on to three months."

"Well, now that you mention it, yore dog died."

"My dog!?! My good hunting dog!?!"

"Yep."

"What happened? That dog was in good shape when I left. How could he die?"

"Well, we ain't exactly shore, but it seemed he choked on some burnt horse flesh."

"Burnt horse flesh!?! Where would he get ahold of burnt horse flesh?"

"When your barn burned down, it got your horse, and then your dog got into the smoking wreckage."

"MY barn burned down?!?"

"Yep. Pretty much to the ground. Then it got your horse and of course, your dog."

"How did my barn catch fire?"

"We think it was the sparks from your house."

"Wait. What?!? My house burned down?!?"

"Yep. Pretty much like your barn, right to the ground."

"How did that happen?"

"We think it was from one of the candles…"

"Now wait just a minute there! I don't allow candles in my house. They're a fire hazard."

"They know that now!"

"Why were there candles?"

"They were in the parlor around the casket."

"THE CASKET!?! Who died?!?"

"Your mother-in-law."

"What happened to her? When I left, she was in pretty good shape, about as good as the huntin' dog."

"We can't be exactly shore, but we think it was the shock of when your wife ran off with that traveling salesman. It got her, the house, the barn, your horse, and your good huntin' dog. But you know, other than that, not a thing has happened since you was gone."

This is a ridiculous tale, but it interests me. Many people who know the Gospel story, the story of Jesus, are like the fellow in the story. When approached, they treat Jesus' story as no news, no news at all.

The *Gospel of John* begins with news about the Word.

The Word is supreme. Everything comes from God's Word. All of creation is called into being through God's Word. Then the writer of *John* shifts to John the Baptizer, who is identified as a testifying witness.

As a kid, that word "witness" was a little confusing to me. I liked to watch the courtroom drama, Perry Mason. I understood that the person who sat in the "witness chair" beside the judge was a "witness." They spoke of what they had seen and heard. So as the witness spoke, he/she "witnessed." But I also knew that when you saw something, you "witnessed" it as well.

So, a witness is someone who witnessed about something they witnessed. (English words can be fun.) No "hearsay" is accepted in court. The person has to have experienced the event about which they are testifying.

In verse 14 of the first chapter, the author, in this wonderful prologue to the book we call The *Gospel of John* wrote, "The Word became flesh and lived among us." Other translations read "moved into the neighborhood," "made his home among us," "moved in with us," "tabernacled (fixed His tent of flesh, lived awhile) among us."

One translation (the Expanded Bible) even says "pitched his tabernacle; God's glorious presence dwelt in Israel's tabernacle in the wilderness." The words used in the passage are "to pitch a tent," which is exactly what the tabernacle in the wilderness was—a large tent.

So, the Word became flesh and pitched a tent alongside us. This is the Good News of Christmas. The Good News of the story of Jesus.

Some years ago, we attended Christmas Eve service with our daughter and her family. We went to the family service in the middle of the afternoon. It was delightful. The entire service was a wiggling, squirming, giggling, whispering, crying, talking affair.

If you were seeking peace and silence for Christmas Eve, this was not the moment to attend. This was a service designed for children and those who love children.

One of the traditions at their church is to construct a nativity scene with wooden figures. As the children enter the sanctuary, they are given a wooden figurine—a shepherd, a wiseman, an angel, a sheep, a camel, a donkey, Mary, Joseph, or the Baby Jesus.

As the old, familiar story is retold, the children bring their pieces to the table in the front at the altar rail. Our oldest granddaughter (who was about four or five) was standing on tiptoes beside me in the pew. As the last piece, Baby Jesus, was brought down the aisle, she leaned against me straining to see. She bent over and whispered, "I would like to see Jesus someday."

Since that time, we have talked about where and how to see the Living Jesus. It was important to me for her to know she did not have to wait to see Jesus, because he lives among us.

One summer at church camp, I was helping counselors work with young children, doing the usual camp activities. Nathaniel, one of our kids that week, had never been to camp before. It was all new to him. Each morning at devotions, the children listened patiently as one of us told a story from the Bible. On the last day, it was my turn. I had prepared the story of Jesus calming the storm, and I wanted to talk to the kids about their fears.

When I began, little Nathaniel interrupted and said, "I know a story!" When I asked what it was, he held up his new Bible (which he had received that week) and said, "This is my story." Nathaniel is a witness to the Word.

As a teen, I attended the Chattanooga District Conference in the position of "youth delegate." At that point in my life, I had not worshiped in diverse settings or communities. The music that day was mostly familiar. The prayers were familiar. It was all pretty similar to my experience—until the sermon began. I should have realized it was going to be different when I sat beside an older black man. He flashed a bright smile at me. "Welcome to church!" he said. During the prayer, he talked! Not very loud or intrusively but talked, nevertheless.

That was nothing compared to what he did during the sermon. He yelled at the preacher who was a bishop! The man shouted, "Tell that Story! Tell that Story! Come on now, tell that story!" That vocal man was a witness whose impassioned words pointed me toward the Word.

Francis Asbury, an early bishop of the Methodist Episcopal Church, traveled through much of the area in which I grew up. Asbury (with three others) struggled to cross the Great Smoky Mountains from Tennessee to North Carolina on November 30, 1810, (the year he was 65 years old). The group of men left before sunrise and traveled all day. They arrived in the small community of Clyde, North Carolina, nearly four hours after sunset. Dark to dark.

The next day, Asbury preached to a small group at Father Shook's house. My grandfather's ancestors heard this preaching. They later moved to distant Alabama where they were charter members at the Methodist church in Moulton, Alabama.

Asbury traveled over 275,000 miles throughout the American frontier. Once he became bishop, part of those total miles was a 4,500-mile annual circuit. Asbury and others of his day were witnesses. The Word resonated in their preaching and their lives of service.

*John* wrote, "The Word became flesh, and lived with us" (1:14). *John* then wrote his version of the amazing life of Jesus that he himself had witnessed. In his storytelling, *John* made Jesus visible to many generations. As the story wound to a close, *John* wrote:

> *Then Jesus did many other miraculous signs in his disciples' presence, signs that aren't recorded in this scroll. But these things are written so that you will believe that Jesus is the Christ, God's Son, and that believing, you will have life in his name.*
>
> **John 20:30-31 (CEB)**

> *Jesus did many other things as well. If all of them were recorded, I imagine the world itself wouldn't have enough room for the scrolls that would be written.*
>
> **John 21:25 (CEB)**

The writer of *John* told Jesus' story in such a compelling manner that the words brought us the Word. Have we told the story of Jesus? Have we witnessed? Or do we guard the Good News of the Gospel, thinking it is no news at all. Have we shared how we met Jesus and how Jesus changed our life?

In the postscript of the *Gospel of John—The Three Letters of John*—we hear:

> *We announce to you what existed from the beginning, what we have heard, what we have seen with our eyes, what we have seen and our hands handled, about the word of life. The life was revealed, and we have seen, and we testify and announce to you the eternal life that was with the Father and was revealed to us. What we have seen and heard, we also announce it to you so that you can have fellowship with us. Our fellowship is with the Father and with his Son, Jesus Christ. We are writing these things so that our joy can be complete.*
>
> *This is the message that we have heard from him and announce to you: "God is light and there is no darkness in him at all." If we claim, "We have fellowship with him," and live in the darkness, we are lying and do not act truthfully. But if we live in the light in the same way as he is in the light, we have fellowship with each other, and the blood of Jesus, his Son, cleanses us from every sin.*
>
> **I John 1:1-7 (CEB)**

Do you remember being taught about the battle of Marathon? In 490 BCE, an army of twenty-thousand

Persians arrived on the shores of Greece in six hundred ships. The Athenians gathered to meet this invasion. Artaphernes and Datis' Persian force outnumbered the Athenian army more than two to one. In an amazing turn, the Athenians (led by Miltiades) routed the Persians who fled to their ships.

The legend tells us that, amid victory celebrations—as the Persian ships were sailing away—the citizens would have seen the ships coming before news of the victory reached Athens. They might have surrendered. A runner, Pheidippides, conquered the twenty-six-plus miles from Marathon to Athens to deliver the news—"Rejoice, we conquer!"—and then fell dead of exhaustion.

Many are giving up because the odds are overwhelming, and they can only see defeat. They need the message, the Good News: Rejoice! He Conquers.

The Word became flesh and lived with us. We are told to take the words of scripture and make them become flesh again. We are to be the good news. We are to make the Word live.

# What is So Little Among So Many?

The only miracle story that appears in all four gospels is the story of Jesus feeding the multitudes, also known as the feeding of the five thousand. Everyone remembers this story. Here is how *John* tells it:

*After this Jesus went across the Galilee Sea (that is, the Tiberias Sea). A large crowd followed him, because they had seen the miraculous signs he had done among the sick. Jesus went up a mountain and sat there with his disciples. It was nearly time for Passover, the Jewish festival.*

*Jesus looked up and saw the large crowd coming toward him. He asked Philip, "Where will we buy food to feed these people?" Jesus said this to test him, for he already knew what he was going to do.*

*Philip replied, "More than a half year's salary[a] worth of food wouldn't be enough for each person to have even a little bit." One of his disciples, Andrew, Simon Peter's brother, said, "A youth here has five barley loaves and two fish. But what good is that for a crowd like this?"*

*Jesus said, "Have the people sit down." There was plenty of grass there. They sat down, about five thousand of them. Then Jesus took the bread. When he had given thanks, he distributed it to those who were sitting there. He did the same with the fish, each getting as much as they wanted. When they had plenty to eat, he said to his disciples, "Gather up the leftover pieces, so that nothing will be wasted." So they gathered them and filled twelve baskets with the pieces of the five barley loaves that had been left over by those who had eaten.*

*When the people saw that he had done a miraculous sign, they said, "This is truly the prophet who is coming into the world." Jesus understood that they were about to come and force him to be their king, so he took refuge again, alone on a mountain.*

**John 6:1-15 (CEB)**

Jesus and the disciples have gone on a retreat away from it all. They crossed the lake and went out into the middle of nowhere, far, far away. However, people have been following Jesus. They have been watching him heal, listening to him speak, gathering around his charismatic personality. When the group on the lake retreat looked up, there they were, a crowd of five thousand! (It really could have been more, since the text says five thousand men—so there were women and children along as well. Who knows how many? Ten thousand or more?)

When Jesus saw them, he had pity on them. Jesus remembered that God fed the people of Israel in the wilderness on their journey to the Promised Land. He was not willing to send them away hungry, so he said, Let's feed them.

Philip said, "You've got to be kidding! We would need two hundred days of wages! Even that amount would only buy enough for each person to have a bite, a crumb! We don't have that kind of resources! What is that among so many? What could we possibly do with so little?

We often hear this passage when we are talking about the church budget. We also hear it when we talk about the big issues. Poverty. Homelessness. Hatred. Racism. War. We have so little to offer! We cannot possibly deal with that!

Andrew, Simon Peter's brother, offered what little was on hand—five barley loaves and two fish—with the observation, What is that little bit among so many?

Jesus is not disturbed. He simply gives instructions. He does not argue with the two disciples. He does not acknowledge the scarcity of resources. He simply says, "Have them sit down."

This is one of those places in scripture when our dependence on translations can fail us. Only a few English translations get this passage right. In verse 10, we hear Jesus say, "Have them sit down." But in Greek, the word that we hear as "sit down" really means "recline" or "lie down."

What Jesus actually said was, "Have them recline." In Jesus' day, the way one ate at a banquet was to recline. This is how the Last Supper was eaten, Jesus and his students reclining around the table. Da Vinci's depiction of the Last Supper was a "translation" for his own day. That was not how the meal looked.

A real picture would have Jesus, the Beloved Disciple on his left and Judas Iscariot on his right, all lying side by side.

When Jesus gave the instruction for the multitudes to recline, he was saying, "This is no picnic! Have them get ready for a banquet!" He was saying, "We are not offering a snack of crumbs but a feast!"

When everyone had their fill, when all had eaten enough, there were leftovers!

*And God is able to provide you with every blessing in abundance, so that by always having enough of everything, you may share abundantly in every good work.*

**II Corinthians 9:8 (NRSV)**

This event in the wilderness is a foretaste (literally a taste) of the Messianic feast that God will offer the nations. Jesus offered the banquet that God provides now and in the future.

My first full-time appointment as a pastor was to New Salem United Methodist Church in a community also known as Plum Nelly. It was called Plum Nelly because it was located in the northwest corner of Georgia atop Lookout Mountain, south of Chattanooga, Tennessee. It was called Plum Nelly because it was "Plum" out of Tennessee and "Nelly" out of Georgia.

The church building was a beautiful structure of mountain stone. To one side stood the parsonage, also of mountain stone, while on the other was a one-hundred-foot-long table about three feet tall, higher than traditional table height. I was curious as to what purpose this long, high table served.

We arrived in the winter, so we were not outside at the table much. Then I was told about the all-day-sing event they held. I asked, "What do we do?" They smiled, "We sing all day." "Yes, but what do I do that day?" "You sing all day!"

When the day came, we sang all day! It was wonderful to hear the congregation sing in four-part harmony and to listen to solos, quartets, and more.

At noon, we went outside for lunch, and then I finally realized the table's purpose. At Plum Nelly, they did not have covered-dish meals. They had covered-basket meals. Everyone brought a couple of baskets of food. Delicious food! The type of food served in heaven!

We always seemed to leave with more food than we brought. The best of the best was served and shared. I do not know how Jesus accomplished the feeding of the multitudes. I only know that Jesus supplied the many with an abundance of food.

Did you read all of verse 10? "Jesus said, 'Have them recline.' There was plenty of grass there." Lie down on the grass. Does this sound familiar? Poetry truly is that which gets lost in the translation. Listen to the beauty and wonder in the way that *John* tells this story.

## Psalm 23

*The Lord is my shepherd, I shall not want.*
　*He makes me lie down in green pastures;*
*he leads me beside still waters;*
　*he restores my soul.*
*He leads me in right paths*
　*for his name's sake.*

*Even though I walk through the darkest valley,*
　*I fear no evil;*
*for you are with me;*
　*your rod and your staff—*
　*they comfort me.*

*You prepare a table before me*
  *in the presence of my enemies;*
*you anoint my head with oil;*
  *my cup overflows.*
*Surely goodness and mercy shall follow me*
  *all the days of my life,*
*and I shall dwell in the house of the Lord*
  *my whole life long.*

**Psalm 23 (NRSV)**

In John 6:11 (CEB), "Jesus took the bread. When he had given thanks, he distributed it to those who were reclining there." Again, the phrasing sounds familiar. Jesus took the bread and gave thanks and broke it. These words are used for the Eucharist, Communion. We remember that Jesus comes with plenty for ALL. This story is marked by abundance. An abundance of food. An abundance of God's love. Too often we are Philip and Andrew who say, "We don't have enough." But Jesus answers with confidence and abundance.

# A Blind Man

*As Jesus walked along, he saw a man who was blind from birth. Jesus' disciples asked, "Rabbi, who sinned so that he was born blind, this man or his parents?"*

*Jesus answered, "Neither he nor his parents. This happened so that God's mighty works might be made visible in him. While it's daytime, we must do the works of him who sent me. Night is coming when no one can work. While I am in the world, I am the light of the world."*

*After he said this, he spit on the ground, made mud with the saliva, and smeared the mud on the man's eyes. Jesus said to him, "Go, wash in the pool of Siloam" (this word means sent). So the man went away and washed. When he returned, he could see.*

*The man's neighbors and those who used to see him when he was a beggar said, "Isn't this the man who used to sit and beg?"*

*Some said, "It is," and others said, "No, it's someone who looks like him."*

*But the man said, "Yes, it's me!"*

*So they asked him, "How are you now able to see?"*

*He answered, "The man they call Jesus made mud, smeared it on my eyes, and said, 'Go to the pool of Siloam and wash.' So I went and washed, and then I could see."*

*They asked, "Where is this man?"*

*He replied, "I don't know."*

*Then they led the man who had been born blind to the Pharisees. Now Jesus made the mud and smeared it on the man's eyes on a Sabbath day. So Pharisees also asked him how he was able to see.*

*The man told them, "He put mud on my eyes, I washed, and now I see."*

*Some Pharisees said, "This man isn't from God, because he breaks the Sabbath law." Others said, "How can a sinner do miraculous signs like these?" So they were divided. Some of the Pharisees questioned the man who had been born blind again: "What do you have to say about him, since he healed your eyes?"*

*He replied, "He's a prophet."*

**John 9:1-17 (CEB)**

Remember that *John* the author also wrote:

*Then Jesus did many other signs in his disciples' presence, signs that aren't recorded in this scroll. But these things are written so that you will believe that Jesus is the Christ, God's Son, and that believing, you will have life in his name.*

**John 20:30-31 (CEB)**

Let's consider the sixth of the signs (a blind man sees) that *John* uses to point to Jesus' true identity. This is one of my favorite stories in *John*. It is so well told. It is fun and revealing. Look at the structure of this story among the larger story of Jesus.

*As he walked along, Jesus saw a man who was blind from birth.*

**John 9:1 (CEB)**

This is my interpretation of John 9:26-41:

Jesus' disciples wanted to have a theological discussion. "What caused this guy's blindness? I mean, after all," they said, "you get what you deserve." "Obviously, he—or maybe his parents—did something to cause this calamity." "It is clear that this person made some bad decisions along the way. If he had lived rightly, he would not be in this condition."

The disciples wanted to have a study group discussion. They wanted to talk about the causes of blindness, of homelessness, of addiction, of racism, of poverty. They didn't even see the man himself. They only saw his condition, his circumstance: he was blind. The disciples ascribed the man's identity to his blindness.

"Evidently, this person did something."

"Plainly, this person sinned for this to happen."

"Unmistakably this person made poor choices, or he wouldn't have been in this predicament."

"But wait!" one of them said, "he was born blind. How could he have done something?"

"Well, then, his parents are the problem."

But the first words of this story are "Jesus saw a man."

Jesus said, "I Am the light of the world. I am he who illuminates. Everyone can see clearly in the full light of day, the new day."

After Jesus spit and made some mud, he rubbed it on the man's eyes. He then sent the man to clean up at the Pool of Siloam. Notice that the man is not immediately healed of his condition. Saliva was seen as having healing powers. (Ask any guy in my fourth-grade class. If we got a cut, a scrape, or a bad bruise, we knew to spit on it. I'm not sure how we knew to do this, but it somehow seemed to help.)

Siloam is the pool from where the water to cleanse the temple was drawn. The man went to Siloam and bathed in these waters. He cleaned the "temple" of his body, and suddenly he could see.

As he was walking around—not being led about, not bumping into things, not stumbling over objects—people noticed. Someone said, "Is that the blind beggar?" "Sure looks like him." "Naw, can't be! I thought I just saw him around the corner begging at his usual spot."

"Yes! It's me!"

"How can it be?"

"Jesus came along and put some mud on me and told me to bathe at Siloam. Now I can see."

The Pharisaical religious leaders said, "This Jesus can't be good. He worked on the Sabbath. The law clearly states that you don't knead dough on the Sabbath."

"Well, it wasn't dough, but the work was the same. Even so, you can't mix mud on the Sabbath to make bricks."

"He didn't make bricks."

"Well then, you weren't blind to begin with."

"Oh, but I was!"

"Bring his parents.

"Is this your son? Was he really born blind? How can he now see?"

"He is our son. He was born blind. But we don't know how this happened. Ask him. He's old enough."

(I like this part. The parents can only see trouble in this exchange. Even if he was their son, they didn't seem to mind throwing him under the donkey cart.)

The Pharisees went back to the healed blind beggar. They told him, "We know that this man who you say healed you is a sinner."

"I don't know whether he is a sinner. Here's what I do know: I was blind and now I see."

They questioned him: "What did he do to you? How did he heal your eyes?"

He replied, "I already told you, and you didn't listen. Why do you want to hear it again? Do you want to become his disciples too?"

They insulted him: "You are his disciple, but we are Moses' disciples. We know that God spoke to Moses, but we don't know where this man is from."

The man answered, "This is incredible! You don't know where he is from, yet he healed my eyes! We know that God doesn't listen to sinners. God listens to anyone who is devout and does God's will. No one has ever heard of a healing of the eyes of someone born blind. If this man wasn't from God, he couldn't do this."

They responded, "You were born completely in sin! How

is it that you dare to teach us?" Then they expelled him.

Jesus heard they had expelled the man born blind. Finding him, Jesus said, "Do you believe in the Human One?"

He answered, "Who is he, sir? I want to believe in him."

Jesus said, "You have seen him. In fact, he is the one speaking with you."

The man said, "Lord, I believe." And he worshiped Jesus.

Jesus said, "I have come into the world to exercise judgment so that those who don't see can see and those who see will become blind."

Some Pharisees who were with him heard what he said and asked, "Surely we aren't blind, are we?"

Jesus said to them, "If you were blind, you wouldn't have any sin, but now that you say, 'We see,' your sin remains.

---

I love this story. The only people who saw clearly are Jesus and the blind guy. Even the disciples didn't see him. They looked past the man to discuss why he was blind. They wanted to study the underlying causes.

Only when Jesus' light shines on the situation do other people start to see something amazing and new. When the light of Jesus shines in our lives, then we begin to see differently. In the light of Jesus, situations are transformed, and we can see a child of God clearly.

In Jesus, we see everything in a whole new light, the light of Jesus. In the light of Jesus, darkness is dispelled. We no longer stumble about in night's darkness. We live in the light of a new day.

※

It was dusk, almost night. We had finished our weekly Bible study looking at the gospels in the New Testament. We climbed the stairs from the basement and stepped out into the gathering darkness. There in the parking lot right in front of the church's entrance was an old Chevy station wagon, bent and rusted. A crusty fellow with a scraggly beard and wearing stained, threadbare clothes got out of the car.

"Can you folks help us? We are driving from Atlanta to Cincinnati and need some help." In the failing light, we could not see inside the car. "Can you fine Christian folks help a man and his family who are down on their luck?"

Jake Jones, a hard worker and veteran of World War II, snorted. He grabbed my arm and said over his shoulder as he dragged me away, "We'll be right back."

I never had to worry about what Jake was thinking. He freely shared his opinions, and I didn't always think he saw things very clearly. For instance, he knew everything there was to know about raising children, but he had never had any of his own.

"He is a dirty skunk!" Jake said. "He's a good-for-nothing con man. He is trying to take advantage of us. Look, nobody drives across the mountain to get anywhere. You don't pass us to go somewhere else. Follow the highway from Atlanta to Cincinnati, you don't get here. He just happened to pass here when we are coming out of Wednesday night Bible study at eight o'clock? A con man is what he is."

When we returned, the scraggly fellow was still talking to some of the church members who were standing in the parking lot. I didn't know what to do. I was a newly minted pastor fresh from the halls of academia. The ink was hardly dry on my seminary diploma, and I had never faced a situation like this.

We offered several solutions: food, gas. The fellow only wanted money. As the man kept talking, two children spilled out of the old station wagon. A little girl in a dirty dress came up beside the man and slipped her hand into his.

I was stammering about what we might do or couldn't do. We didn't keep any cash at the church, and I had very little on me. I hated to force my new parishioners into an unexpected offering. Suddenly Jake said, "Wait just a minute!" He lowered his voice as he spoke in my ear, "I'll take them down to Trenton and pay for them to sleep in Cloudland Inn."

I was confused. "What? Wait, I thought you said he is a low-down skunk, that he is a con man!"

"He is," said Jake, "but those kids can't help that. They need a clean, safe place to stay the night. You keep telling us Jesus loves everybody! Don't you think Jesus loves them kids and even that old skunk?"

My last memory from that night is the beams of Jake's headlights cutting into the dark leading the car of the con man and his family to a safe, clean place.

Jake was the only one who saw clearly. He saw and understood the need.

Jake brought out the light of Jesus, and we could all see better.

In John 9, the only person who sees is the man born blind. Only the blind man sees in the light of Jesus. Enjoy the irony of this well-told story.

# The Heart and Mind of Christ

*As the Father loved me, I too have loved you. Remain in my love. If you keep my commandments, you will remain in my love, just as I kept my Father's commandments and remain in his love. I have said these things to you so that my joy will be in you and your joy will be complete. This is my commandment: love each other just as I have loved you. No one has greater love than to give up one's life for one's friends. You are my friends if you do what I command you. I don't call you servants any longer, because servants don't know what their master is doing. Instead, I call you friends, because everything I heard from my Father I have made known to you. You didn't choose me, but I chose you and appointed you so that you could go and produce fruit and so that your fruit could last. As a result, whatever you ask the Father in my name, he will give you. I give you these commandments so that you can love each other.*

**John 15:9-17 (CEB)**

## "The Magic Lifesaving Stick"

*Once upon a time, Rabbit was traveling along and met up with his friend, Porcupine. "Where are you going?" asked Porcupine. "I'm going home," answered Rabbit. "Where is home?" inquired Porcupine.*

*"Oh, it's a long way from here—across a river, over a swamp, through a forest, and up on a high mountain."*

*"I've always heard that if you take a friend along, it*

*will shorten a journey."*

*"That sounds good to me. Would you like to go along?"*

*"I would love to go with you."*

*The two creatures had traveled along for a short time when they rounded a curve in the trail and tripped over a stick. Wham! They both fell flat on their faces.*

*Rabbit stood up, brushed himself off, and started to throw the stick aside when Porcupine said, "Wait. Let me see that."*

*"Why?" asked Rabbit.*

*"It might be a magic lifesaving stick."*

*"Oh, don't be ridiculous. It fell off that tree, down in the trail, and tripped us. Let's get it out of the way and be off."*

*"I'll keep it. It might be a special."*

*"Suit yourself," said Rabbit.*

*Off the two creatures went, Rabbit hopping along and Porcupine carrying his new stick.*

*They came to the river. You and I would call it a creek, but these were small animals, and they saw it as a river.*

*"How will we get across?" asked Porcupine.*

*"Oh, that's easy," said Rabbit. He went back a bit and then hop, hop, hop – jumped over the creek.*

*"Wait! I'm not built like you!" said Porcupine.*

*"Well, I've enjoyed traveling with you, but I'm going home."*

*"Wait. Let me think about it." Porcupine hefted the stick in his paws, backed up, and then ran as fast as his little legs would carry him. He stuck the stick in the creek and pole vaulted to the other side.*

"Wow. That stick is amazing. It really is magic," said Rabbit.

"I told you."

The two creatures continued on their way. When they came to the swamp, Porcupine used the stick to find firm places to stand and soggy places to avoid.

"Oh, that will take too long," said Rabbit. "I'll meet you on the other side."

And off he went. Hop, hop, hop, splash. "Help, help! I'm drowning!"

Porcupine used the stick and reached out to Rabbit just as he was going under for the last time. He pulled him from the water. "Whew," Rabbit said. "You saved me with that stick. It really is a magic lifesaving stick."

"I told you," smiled Porcupine.

They continued on and came to the forest. It was a thick, dense forest. "How can we go now?" said Rabbit. "We can't see the trail."

"Oh, that's easy," replied Porcupine. He took the stick and stuck it into the dense undergrowth, pushing the brush aside. "See, there's the trail right there." He used the stick this way until they reached a small clearing in the middle of the forest. There sat Wolf. Wolf looked up and grinned, "Lunch!"

Porcupine balled up and showed his quills. Wolf said, "I'm not interested in you." And then he put his paw on Rabbit.

"Help!" Rabbit cried. "I'm going to be his lunch!" Porcupine got up and struck Wolf across the tail with the stick. "Yi! Yi! Yi!" Wolf screamed as he ran away.

"Come on, let's get out of here," Rabbit said. "He may have brothers." The two creatures hurried on.

*They came to the foot of a high mountain. As they stared up to its heights toward the sky, Rabbit said, "We'll never make it now! I'm exhausted!"*

*Porcupine held out the stick. "Here. Hold on to the other end, and I'll hold on to this end. When you get tired, I'll help you along, and when I get tired, you can help me." And so, side by side, holding on to the stick, they helped each other up the mountain.*

*When they got to the top, they went over to the tree where Rabbit's burrow was. "I'm home!" he shouted.*

*All the rabbit children came out, and came out, and came out, and came out – after all, he was a rabbit. Mrs. Rabbit said, "Where have you been?" Not really. She used those words but not that tone. "WHERE HAVE YOU BEEN?!?!"*

*Rabbit told her all their adventures and everywhere they had been and said, "We wouldn't be here today if it weren't for Porcupine's magic lifesaving stick."*

*"Oh, with so many children, I wish I had a magic lifesaving stick," she said.*

*Porcupine said, "Well, here, you can have mine."*

*"Oh, no. I could not take yours. Then you wouldn't have one."*

*"That's okay," said Porcupine. "I'll just find another stick."*

*"But what if it isn't a magic lifesaving stick?"*

*"Don't worry. Any stick will do," Porcupine said. "Because the magic isn't in the stick. It is here (as he touched his heart) and here (as he touched his head).*

**Based on an old Russian folk tale**

People spend their entire lives searching for a magic lifesaving stick. The perfect job. The perfect church. The perfect pastor. The perfect friend. The perfect spouse.

They never realize that the magic is not in the stick but in the heart and mind of Christ.

> *This is my commandment: love each other just as I have loved you. No one has greater love than to give up one's life for one's friends.*
>
> **John 15:12-13 (CEB)**

This type of love requires both our hearts and our minds. After all, that is the commandment Jesus had heard from his birth.

> *Israel, listen! Our God is the Lord! Only the Lord!*
>
> *Love the Lord your God with all your heart, all your being, and all your strength. These words that I am commanding you today must always be on your minds. Recite them to your children. Talk about them when you are sitting around your house and when you are out and about, when you are lying down and when you are getting up. Tie them on your hand as a sign. They should be on your forehead as a symbol. Write them on your house's doorframes and on your city's gates.*
>
> **Deuteronomy 6:4-9 (CEB)**

Any love that involves God requires everything of us. To love like Jesus is to be all in.

Listen to the wedding ceremony. The question is not "Do you love each other?" The question is "Will you love each other?"

"Will you love each other?" To love in a marriage requires a decision, an act of the will. Will you love each other for better or worse, in sickness and in health, for richer or poorer? We do not ask, Do you like each other? Do you have things in common?

Love requires an act of will, a decision. Love requires our mind. We decide each and every day to love our spouse.

Perhaps you have heard the old joke about a man who had a rare brain disease. His doctor told him, "You have a rare brain disease, and it is 100 percent fatal. There is no known cure."

The man was shocked. "But doctor, surely there is something you can do. You aren't giving me any hope. I'm a young man to have such a death sentence."

"There is no known cure," the doctor said. "But there is a brand-new treatment that might work."

"Doc, it doesn't matter what it is. I'll try it if it is my only hope. What is it?"

"Well...it's a brain transplant."

"A brain transplant!?! I've never heard of such a thing!"

"It's brand new. Cutting edge. But I need to warn you. You get what you pay for."

"What do you mean?"

"Here's a Baptist brain," said the doctor. "It's five thousand dollars."

"Five thousand dollars! Why so much?"

"Well, it's saved, and you have to pay for that. Now here is a Presbyterian brain. It's ten thousand dollars."

"Ten thousand dollars! Why so much?"

"Well, it's predestined, and you have to pay for that. There's one more back here in the vault. It's a Methodist brain. Twenty-five thousand dollars."

"Twenty-five thousand dollars! My goodness! Why so much?"

"Well, it's never been used," the doctor said.

Surely, we don't want that said about us! We are commanded to love with our heart, mind, soul, and strength. We must decide to love, the way a parent decides to love a child. There you are lying in bed at two a.m., and the baby starts to cry. You say, "It's your turn to love the baby."

Loving a baby requires a decision, not just every day but all the time. Then you get past the infancy stage and hit the terrible twos. Later, the child becomes a teenager, and you must decide all over again.

It's not a chore to love people we like. Anyone can do that. Jesus talked about loving others as he loved. He said to love your enemies, the people you don't like. The people who don't like you.

What does this mean? How do we love our neighbors? How do we love our enemies?

"Love as I love you." We are to love in right ways, the ways that Jesus loves. Indiscriminately, personally, gracefully. We are to love one-on-one.

Linus and Lucy in the Peanuts comic strip were arguing one day. Lucy told her brother, Linus, that he could not be a doctor because he didn't love mankind, to which Linus replied, "I love mankind! It's people I can't stand!"

Loving like Jesus loves brings us joy, the complete joy of God in Jesus.

A sequel to the *Gospel of John* is *I John*. Listen to how *John* writes to the church to remind them of the teachings of Jesus:

> *Don't be surprised, brothers and sisters, if the world hates you. We know that we have transferred from death to life, because we love the brothers and sisters. The person who does not love remains in death. Everyone who hates a brother or sister is a murderer, and you know that murderers don't have eternal life residing in them. This is how we know love: Jesus laid down his life for us, and we ought to lay down our lives for our brothers and sisters. But if someone has material possessions and sees a brother or sister in need but refuses to help—how can the love of God dwell in a person like that? Little children, let's not love with words or speech but with action and truth. This is how we will know that we belong to the truth and reassure our hearts in God's presence.*
>
> *This is his commandment, that we believe in the name of his Son, Jesus Christ, and love each other as he commanded us. Those who keep his commandments dwell in God and God dwells in them. This is how we know that he dwells in us, because of the Spirit he has given us.*
>
> **I John 3:13-19; 23-24 (CEB)**

We are to love with action and truth. We are to love with the heart and mind of Christ.

> *I've loved you the way my Father has loved me. Make yourselves at home in my love. If you keep my commands, you'll remain intimately at home in my love. That's what I've done—kept my Father's commands and made myself at home in his love.*
>
> *I've told you these things for a purpose: that my joy might be your joy, and your joy wholly mature. This is my command: Love one another the way I loved you. This is the very best way to love. Put your life on the line for your friends. You are my friends when you do the things I command you. I'm no longer calling you servants because servants don't understand what their master is thinking and planning. No, I've named you friends because I've let you in on everything I've heard from the Father.*
>
> *"You didn't choose me, remember; I chose you, and put you in the world to bear fruit, fruit that won't spoil. As fruit bearers, whatever you ask the Father in relation to me, he gives you.*
>
> *But remember the root command: Love one another.*
>
> **John 15:9-17 (MSG)**

The magic is not in the stick. It is in the heart and mind of Jesus Christ.

# The Comforter

*"If you love me, you will keep my commandments. I will ask the Father, and he will send another Companion, who will be with you forever. This Companion is the Spirit of Truth, whom the world can't receive because it neither sees him nor recognizes him. You know him, because he lives with you and will be with you.*

*"I won't leave you as orphans. I will come to you. Soon the world will no longer see me, but you will see me. Because I live, you will live too. On that day you will know that I am in my Father, you are in me, and I am in you. Whoever has my commandments and keeps them loves me. Whoever loves me will be loved by my Father, and I will love them and reveal myself to them."*

*Judas (not Judas Iscariot) asked, "Lord, why are you about to reveal yourself to us and not to the world?"*

*Jesus answered, "Whoever loves me will keep my word. My Father will love them, and we will come to them and make our home with them. Whoever doesn't love me doesn't keep my words. The word that you hear isn't mine. It is the word of the Father who sent me.*

*"Peace I leave with you. My peace I give you. I give to you not as the world gives. Don't be troubled or afraid. You have heard me tell you, 'I'm going away and returning to you.' If you loved me, you would be happy that I am going to the Father, because the Father is greater than me. I have told you before it happens so that when it happens you will believe. I won't say much more to you because this world's ruler is coming. He has nothing on me. Rather, he comes so that the world will know that I love the Father and do just as the Father has commanded me. Get up. We're leaving this place.*

**John 14:15-31 (CEB)**

*And I will ask the Father, and He will give you another Helper (Comforter, Advocate, Intercessor—Counselor, Strengthener, Standby), to be with you forever.*

**John 14:16 (AMP)**

*And I will pray the Father, and he shall give you another Comforter, that he may abide with you for ever.*

**John 14:16 (KJV)**

As fun as a week of church camp can be, it may not be the best way to spend your third week of marriage. My wife and I volunteered to be co-directors for an entire week of elementary school camp in the Blue Ridge Mountains of southwestern Virginia. Somehow it sounded like a good idea when we volunteered, but as we prepared to be with 50 fourth, fifth, and sixth graders for an entire week within the first month of our marriage, we had second thoughts.

Our camping efforts at the time consisted of an entire staff of volunteers—parents, pastors, high school seniors, college students, and well-meaning people. You need counselors, cooks, cleaners, crafts, games, lessons, plans, contingency plans, plans for when the contingency plans fail, rain plans.

Our home for the week was Camp Ahistadi, just off the road from Damascus, Virginia, on the way to Mountain City, Tennessee. We were so far back in a mountain holler the locals said you couldn't get the Grand Ole Opry's Saturday night broadcast until Tuesday morning. The sun didn't rise until nine and set at three.

It was your typical church camp but set on National

Forest land. Our "pool" was where we piled rocks to dam up Laurel Creek. We used a wild grapevine for a swing and played games out in the field by the creek. There were four cabins where we slept and a lodge where we ate. Our worship center was in the woods with a small rock stack and a log cross behind it.

Every camp in America has a camp ghost story, and Camp Ahistadi was no different. The spooky tale was called "The Legend of Cabin Five." Like most camp ghost stories, it was invented by frustrated, sleep-deprived counselors who could not imagine one more night of kids staying awake until dawn with pranks, trips to the bathhouse, and general restlessness. Failing anything else, they invented a story to scare kids into silent submission.

The scary legend begins with a group of unruly children who were assigned to Cabin Five. The children would not stay in bed and would not let anyone else get any sleep. On Thursday night, the last night of camp that week, a terrible storm rolled up the valley into Ahistadi Holler. Lightning flashed. Thunder shook the earth. A jagged bolt of high-voltage electricity struck Cabin Five and killed all the children until the creek ran with "Bluuuud!!!" You had to say it that way for the full effect of the story. "BLUUUUD!!!" The story continued. "And if you don't stay in bed and behave, it might happen again."

The odd thing was there really had been a Cabin Five, and it really had burned down. No one was hurt. It was a faulty wiring thing. No one was around when it burned, but the wreckage of the old cabin was still visible. Unfortunately, kids could walk through the woods and see the burned timbers now covered with vines and saplings.

It was a HORRIBLE, terrifying story. I have told stories at camps for many years but do not tell ghost stories. If you do it right (and I would want to), they scare people. I'm not really into scaring people. So, when our staff gathered together on Sunday evening, I said, "Does everyone know the Legend of Cabin Five?"

"Yes." "Sure." "Of course, we've been coming to this camp for years!" "Everybody knows the Legend of Cabin Five."

"Great," I said. "DON'T TELL IT! It's a horrible story, and it will just scare the kids. When they go home, that's all they will talk about. Their parents will say, 'Did you learn anything at camp?' And their children will respond, 'Yes, we learned about Cabin Five—lightning, thunder, BLUUUD!'"

"So, no Cabin Five?" they asked.

"Correct! No Cabin Five!"

"Okay, Charles. Calm down. We get it. No Cabin Five."

After this discussion, we went over the week's schedule, the Bible study, the activities, and then we prayed. We took the list of children and prayed for each camper individually. At elementary camp, you have some children coming to camp for the first time. Some were even leaving home overnight for the first time, and some were traveling long distances through the mountains. We remembered each girl and boy by name.

As I remember it, they were the usual kid names: Donny, Susan, Billy, Johnny, Megan—except for one. It leapt off the page. *Jonat han Hooser.* Jonat han Hooser. It didn't have a southwestern Virginia ring to it. We talked about this name for a few minutes and decided he might be one of those foreign-exchange kids.

You know how you can sign up for an exchange program where you mail your kid overseas and they mail you one back? From the sound of his name, we decided he was from Holland. We were excited to have an international visitor as one of our campers, and we knew it would be easy to spot him the next morning. He would have a Dutch-boy haircut with bangs, be wearing wooden shoes, and he obviously would have a swollen finger from the whole leaky dike episode. Lastly, we prayed for little Jonat han Hooser, who was coming all the way across the Atlantic to Camp Ahistadi.

With that, we all went to our bunks. I kissed my new bride as we went to our separate beds in the girls' and boys' cabins.

The next morning, we were up and moving early. We had breakfast together, and I reminded the counselors one more time: "NO CABIN FIVE!" Eyes rolled, but all silently nodded.

Before the children started arriving with their parents, we engaged in last-minute preparations. As they came, they registered at a table outside the lodge. We helped them get their sleeping bags and luggage into the right cabins and introduced them to their counselors.

One small boy came up wearing a large football jersey that went below his knees. His name was Donny Ritchie. He was excited to be at camp, and it showed! He was in constant motion and activity. He wiggled, ran, jumped, wiggled, talked, laughed. He could not stand still as we tried to check him in. His mother hugged him and said, "Have a good week, Donny," to which he replied, "Have a good week, Mommy." She smiled happily and said, "Oh, I will!" With a little too much enthusiasm, she winked at the counselor and said, "Good luck!"

Donny's jersey had his name on the back above the number. It was supposed to say, D RITCHIE. I don't know if he got it at a discount T-shirt shop or what, but the spacing of the letters was off. The space was not between the "D" and "R" but between the "R" and the "I." It spelled "DR ITCHIE."

Children are very observant. Someone spotted the error, and they shouted, "Hey, Dr. Itchie!" The child loved his new nickname. He was so excited. In fact, he wore the shirt the entire week. By the end of the week, the shirt smelled so strong, it was putting him on in the morning instead of the other way around.

Dr. Itchie was one of our children.

Next, a beautiful little girl arrived. Dark curls framed an angelic face with rosy cheeks. To complete the picture, her name was Dawn Rose. What a lovely name for an angelic child. This impression persisted until she spoke. Her voice was like an alley cat on the prowl. The tone was so grating, it could peel paint off walls, and unfortunately, her personality matched her voice. You truly could not judge that book by its cover.

It didn't matter what you said, she was against it. You could have said, "Hey, Dawn, let's have ice cream." "Aww! It'll just melt and get all over my clothes and make me sticky!"

You could have enthusiastically suggested, "Hey, Dawn, let's go swimming!" "Swimming?!? In THAT mud hole?!? There's snakes and frogs down there!" It did not matter what you said, she was not for it!

Dawn Rose, too, was one of our children.

Finally, all the kids had arrived. I stopped by the check in table and was told, "They are all here except that Dutch kid."

"Well, it's a long way from Holland. He may have gotten hung up in New York or was stuck in traffic in Damascus."

"Maybe. But we do have an extra kid who wasn't on the list."

"An extra kid? That's odd. What's his name?"

"Jonathan Houser."

Hmmm. Jonat han Hooser. Jonathan Houser. It was obvious that the old district typewriter had put a "Tuh" and "Huh" where there should have been a "THHH". And of course, "o" and "u" are up on the top row of keys near each other, easily transposed. So, there was our "Dutch kid": Jonathan Houser.

He was a big kid for fifth grade, and he had taken an early growth spurt. His voice was a deep raspy foghorn. You could hear him all over camp!

"Jonat han Hooser" was one of our kids.

We got things moving. At lunch, the day's schedule seemed to be humming along. But by supper, I was beginning to get a little worried. I heard snips of conversation from kids that included words like, "lightning," "thunder," "BLUUUUD!" I was very frustrated. Before we finished supper, I asked all the counselors to meet me on the porch.

"I thought we agreed to not tell 'The Legend of Cabin Five!'" I said.

"Cool down, Charles. We didn't tell it. None of us have uttered one word about it. It's those sixth-grade evangelists who have been here before. They've been spreading the word."

It was too late by then. The story was out. "Lightning! Thunder! BLUUUUD!"

You could hear the campers as they walked through the woods. "Cabin One, Cabin Two, Cabin Three, Cabin Four." Then in hushed, reverent tones, "Cabin Fiiive."

We pushed on. But that night, as we were getting ready for bed after evening devotions, there it was—"Lightning! Thunder! BLUUUUD!" and then a whispered, "Cabin Five." Needless to say, we didn't get much sleep.

Tuesday dawned bright and early. We jumped into our planned activities, and it seemed to go well. We played dodgeball, volleyball, and kickball in the field, and some of the small groups splashed around in the creek swimming hole. After supper and devotions, I led a star study, which was only mildly successful. Given the steepness of the ridges, it was like looking at the sky from the bottom of a well. You could only see the stars straight overhead.

Then came another attempt at getting folks settled for the night with more scattered talk of "Lightning! Thunder! BLUUUUD!" and a whispered, "Cabin Five."

Tuesday night, I lay there waiting for the sound every counselor wants to hear—regular breathing—so you would know everyone was asleep. Then I heard it way in the distance, a low rumble of thunder. My prayer life took a leap forward at that moment. "Oh, Lord! Please not tonight! Let it go somewhere else. Let it storm on the junior high camp next week. Just not tonight."

In the complete darkness, a little voice from the bunk beside mine said, "Charlie?" It was Dr. Itchie.

"Yes."

"Did you hear that?"

"No," I lied.

"Do you think it's thunder?"

"No," I lied again.

"Well, just in case it is...if you are one of those people who gets scared in a storm, it's okay if you want to hold my hand."

"I think I would like that." So, I reached out in the

dark and held that smaller hand. Oddly, the bigger hand seemed a lot sweatier than the small one. The storm went up another valley and stayed away from us. Eventually, the little hand went limp, and I slept fitfully for a second long night.

Wednesday brought rain. We had to make different plans and think up things to do all day with fifty-plus children inside. Seemed like every time we can up with a new idea, Dawn Rose said, "Naw, that's stupid! We hate that game. Can't we do something else?" Wednesday added days to the week and took years off our lives.

The post devotion bedtime ritual still involved grumblings of "Lightning! Thunder! BLUUUUD!" and whispers of "Cabin Five."

Thursday arrived with better weather, but the undercurrent at camp was all about Cabin Five. "Lightning! Thunder! BLUUUUD!"

I was very frustrated. I imagined what Friday morning was going to be like with all the parents coming to pick up their children.

"Did you have a good time?" a mother will ask.

And with bloodshot eyes from no sleep all night, the child says, "Lightning! Thunder! BLUUUUD!" and whispers, "Cabin Five."

"Did you learn anything about Jesus?"

"No, Lightning! Thunder! BLUUUUD!" and whispers, "Cabin Five."

Etc., Etc., Etc.

We finally made it to supper and then to vespers at the outdoor chapel. We sang a few songs, and I presented our evening devotions. As we walked back to the lodge through the gathering darkness in the woods, I realized that all the children were holding hands and oozing down the trail as one large blob. I had never seen fifty children travel in this manner.

There was no way we were going to get any sleep. Several of the leaders and counselors got together. One of them said, "I know. Let's tell a bedtime story."

I thought it couldn't hurt. We weren't going to sleep anytime soon anyway. After all, it was Thursday night, the last night of camp, the night of Cabin Five's gory demise.

"Okay, let's get everyone onto the porch of the lodge."

We gathered the children. The young counselor who had suggested storytelling stepped up. "Would you like to hear a story?"

Most heads nodded.

"Would you like to hear a GHOST story?"

I thought, "What is he doing?!?!? How is this a good idea? It's a ghost story that got us into this whole mess! How will this be helpful?"

But all the children said, "Uh huh," as they slowly nodded their heads.

The counselor continued. "I only believe in one ghost. It's the Holy Ghost." Then he told the story of a dark night when Jesus had supper with his disciples, and no one knew what was going to happen next.

"Jesus told his friends, 'Don't be afraid. I won't leave you without parents. I will send you another, a Comforter.' Do you know what a comforter is?"

"Yes!" Dawn Rose rasped. "It's a blanket!" She knew where he was going and wasn't going to let him get there.

"That's right, Dawn, a blanket."

Jonat han Hooser spoke up, "You mean like a quilt?"

"Yes, a quilt!"

"Ooo, Ooo! I know! I know!" said Dr. Itchie. "My momma and grandmomma make quilts all the time. It's just a bunch of scraps all sewed together."

"Yes! What do you use a quilt for?"

"They keep you warm on a cold night, duh," huffed Dawn.

"Ooo, Ooo! My momma has a purdy one hanging on the wall that we can look at with our eyes, NOT our hands," said Dr. Itchie.

"Yes, sometimes quilts are just beautiful to look at."

Jonat han Hooser chimed in. "You can hide underneath a quilt if there's a monster in your room."

"Right, a quilt can make you feel safe when you're scared. That's what Jesus said he would give to his friends. A comforter, like a quilt to keep you warm when it's cold outside. It can be beautiful when there's ugly around and keep you safe when you're scared. Jesus said he would give his friends a comforter—the

Holy Spirit, the Holy Ghost. And that's the only ghost that I believe in."

The children sat there staring in silence.

"Now let's go to bed and sleep under that comforter tonight."

All the kids breathed, "Whew," and went off to their cabins. We all slept soundly until morning.

The next day as we were corralling children and getting them to their parents, I heard snippets of conversation.

"Hey, Mom, did you know there's a ghost story in the Bible?"

"You know. A comforter, like a quilt—to keep you warm and snuggly."

---

I enjoy the image of the Comforter as a quilt, and the church as a patchwork quilt. A bunch of old scraps bound together by the thread of the Spirit. (Look around any church. There are plenty of old scraps.) As people of the Spirit, we are called to offer warmth to a cold world, beauty to an ugly world, and comfort for a scared world.

# Fanning the Flames

*It was still the first day of the week. That evening, while the disciples were behind closed doors because they were afraid of the Jewish authorities, Jesus came and stood among them. He said, "Peace be with you." After he said this, he showed them his hands and his side. When the disciples saw the Lord, they were filled with joy. Jesus said to them again, "Peace be with you. As the Father sent me, so I am sending you." Then he breathed on them and said, "Receive the Holy Spirit. If you forgive anyone's sins, they are forgiven; if you don't forgive them, they aren't forgiven."*

**John 20:19-23 (CEB)**

We shivered on a cold, cold evening. We had walked all afternoon during our first backpacking adventure as Scouts. We set up camp near the bluff with a view off the mountain across the Great Valley of the Tennessee. Russell, Jimmy, and I pitched our three-man tent and then collected wood for a fire. As it grew darker and colder, we struggled to get a fire going. In our youthful eagerness to create a big fire, we piled log upon log, stick upon stick. We started the fire, but we couldn't seem to keep the flame going.

My Uncle Phil, who was one of our scoutmasters, came over. He shook his head and quietly took our logs apart. He arranged twigs in a pile no larger than his two hands. I didn't see how this would help. We were freezing! We needed a big fire.

He started with a small flame and leaned down to softly blow on it. Slowly but surely, the fire caught and grew. He patiently continued feeding it until it was ablaze. He turned to us and said, "Keep feeding it," and quietly walked away.

---

It was a dark, dark night. Much had happened since dawn. Mary Magdalene had gone to the tomb in the pre-dawn dark and found the stone rolled away. She ran to the disciples and told Simon Peter, "They have taken the Lord out of the tomb." There was a race to the tomb. Simon Peter and the other disciple, the one whom Jesus loved, looked in the tomb and found nothing.

Mary lingered and had an encounter with someone in the garden. At first, she thought it was a gardener, but when he called her by name, she recognized him. The day was long and confusing. No one knew what to think or do.

Finally, it was night again. As the darkness grew, the small group of Jesus' followers became fearful and locked the doors. Then, within their midst, Jesus stood among them. "Peace be with you," he said. Then Jesus showed them his wounds so they would know it was truly him. Next, he breathed on them.

John Wesley, in his *Explanatory Notes on the New Testament,* said that Jesus "breathed new life and vigor" on them.

After that, Jesus sent them out with the words, "Go forth."

Luke, in writing the Acts of the Apostles, used the image of flames and wind, but *John* says Jesus "breathed" on the disciples. The word for *breath* in Greek (and Hebrew, for that matter) is the same as *spirit* and *wind*.

Jesus took a small group of people and breathed on them. He gave them the Holy Spirit and thus set them afire.

Our job as the church is to gather together as kindling for the fire of God's Holy Spirit imparted by Jesus to those first followers.

What is this kindling?

## Personal fire – Wesley at Aldersgate

> *In the evening I went very unwillingly to a society in Aldersgate Street, where one was reading Luther's preface to the Epistle to the Romans. About a quarter before nine, while he was describing the change which God works in the heart through faith in Christ, I felt my heart strangely warmed. I felt I did trust in Christ, Christ alone, for salvation; and an assurance was given me that He had taken away my sins, even mine, and saved me from the law of sin and death.*
>
> *I began to pray with all my might for those who had in a more especial manner despitefully used me and persecuted me. I then testified openly to all there what I now first felt in my heart. But it was not long before the enemy suggested, "This cannot be faith; for where is thy joy?" Then was I taught that peace and victory over sin are essential to faith in the Captain of our salvation; but that, as to the transports of joy that usually attend the beginning of it, especially in those who have mourned*

*deeply, God sometimes giveth, sometimes withholdeth, them according to the counsels of His own will.*

*After my return home, I was much buffeted with temptations, but I cried out, and they fled away. They returned again and again. I as often lifted up my eyes, and He "sent me help from his holy place." And herein I found the difference between this and my former state chiefly consisted. I was striving, yea, fighting with all my might under the law, as well as under grace. But then I was sometimes, if not often, conquered; now, I was always conqueror.*

**John Wesley, May 24, 1738**

At another point in his career, Wesley listed the "kindling" for the fire as three simple rules.

- Do No Harm
- Do Good
- Stay in Love with God

---

*Congregation, then, is no longer the sum of all those who are registered as members on the church rolls. Congregation is rather a new kind of living together for human beings that affirms:*

- *that no one is alone with his or her problems,*
- *that no one has to conceal his or her disabilities*
- *that there are not some who have a say and others who have nothing to say*

- *that neither the old nor the little ones are isolated*
- *that one bears the other even when it is unpleasant and there is no agreement, and*
- *that, finally, the one can also at times leave the other in peace when the other needs it.*

**Jurgen Moltmann**[15]

---

> *Catch on fire with enthusiasm and people will come for miles to watch you burn*
>
> **John Wesley**

Moltmann went on to say, "Acceptance is the atmosphere of humanity. Where acceptance is lacking, the air becomes thin, our breathing falters, and we languish."

The way to put out a fire is to spread the embers out. To separate the fuel. Divide it up. Deprive it of oxygen, atmosphere.

Once while getting our phone service changed, a friend and I chatted with the young women who waited on us. "Holston?" she said. "Is that Methodist? I really loved going to Resurrection each winter when I was in middle and high school."

"Really? What church do you go to?"

"I used to be Methodist. But now, I go to a nondenominational church in Kingsport."

"Do you live in Kingsport?" we asked.

---

15 Jurgen Moltmann, *Passion for Life*, Fortress Press, p. 33.

"No, I drive up there. I go because it's like Resurrection every Sunday. The people at my home church were—well, too content, too cold."

---

It is interesting to me that Jesus linked our sending forth with our ability to forgive. Our "catching fire" had to do with our willingness to engage with others—forgiving ourselves and them as well.

> *Mean laughter went about the town that day*
> *To let him know we weren't the least imposed on,*
> *And he could wait—we'd see to him tomorrow.*
> *But the first thing next morning we reflected*
> *If one by one we counted people out*
> *For the least sin, it wouldn't take us long*
> *To get so we had no one left to live with.*
> *For to be social is to be forgiving.*
>
> **Excerpt from *The Star-splitter* by Robert Frost**

I once heard marriage described as being like a family of porcupines—close enough to stay warm on a cold winter's night but not so close that we needle each other.

Elton Trueblood called the church, "The Incendiary Fellowship."

*Evangelism occurs when people are so enkindled by contact with the central fire of Christ that they, in turn, set others on fire. The only adequate evidence that anything is on fire is the pragmatic evidence that other fires are starting by it. A fire that does not spread must eventually go out! This is the point of Emil Brunner's dictum that "the Church exists by mission as fire exists by burning." A person who claims to have a religious experience, yet makes no effort to share or to extend it, has not really entered into Christ's Company at all. In short, an unevangelistic or unmissionary Christianity is a contradiction in terms.*

**Elton Trueblood**[16]

## Baptism By Fire

*You, whose purpose is to kindle:
Now ignite us with Your fire;
While the earth awaits Your burning
With Your passion us inspire.
Overcome our sinful calmness,
Rouse us with redemptive shame;
Baptize with Your fiery Spirit,
Crown our lives with tongues of flame.*

*You, who, in Your holy Gospel,
Wills that we should truly live:
Make us sense our share of failure,
Our tranquility forgive.
Teach us courage as we struggle*

---

16 Elton Trueblood, *The Incendiary Fellowship,* Harper & Row Publishers, p. 111.

*In all liberating strife;*
*Lift the smallness of our vision,*
*By Your own abundant life.*

*You, who still a sword delivers,*
*Rather than a placid peace:*
*With Your sharpened word disturb us,*
*From complacency, release!*
*Save us now from satisfaction,*
*When we privately are free,*
*Yet are undisturbed in spirit,*
*By our brother's misery.*

**By Elton Trueblood**
(Sung to the tune of "Hyfrydol")

---

Once, my wife and I backpacked on the Appalachian Trail. We got a late start with plans to meet friends at a gap some five-and-a-half miles distant. We left the highway and trekked over two high, grassy balds. We ran out of day before we ran out of trail. We trudged for hours in the dark and cold. Finally, from the summit of the last bald, we looked down to the gap where we had agreed to connect with our group. There, far below, we saw a sparkle of orange light—a small campfire.

When we arrived, we were welcomed to the warmth, the light, a meal, laughter, and hugs. That campfire rendezvous provides a wonderful image of the church.

# Breakfast on the Beach

*Later, Jesus himself appeared again to his disciples at the Sea of Tiberias. This is how it happened: Simon Peter, Thomas (called Didymus), Nathanael from Cana in Galilee, Zebedee's sons, and two other disciples were together. Simon Peter told them, "I'm going fishing."*

*They said, "We'll go with you." They set out in a boat, but throughout the night, they caught nothing. Early in the morning, Jesus stood on the shore, but the disciples didn't realize it was Jesus.*

*Jesus called to them, "Children, have you caught anything to eat?"*

*They answered him, "No."*

*He said, "Cast your net on the right side of the boat and you will find some."*

*So they did, and there were so many fish that they couldn't haul in the net. Then the disciple whom Jesus loved said to Peter, "It's the Lord!" When Simon Peter heard it was the Lord, he wrapped his coat around himself (for he was naked) and jumped into the water. The other disciples followed in the boat, dragging the net full of fish, for they weren't far from shore, only about one hundred yards.*

*When they landed, they saw a charcoal fire there, with fish on it, and some bread. Jesus said to them, "Bring some of the fish that you've just caught." Simon Peter got up and pulled the net to shore. It was full of large fish, one hundred fifty-three of them. Yet the net hadn't torn, even with so many fish. Jesus said to them, "Come and have breakfast." None of the disciples could bring themselves to ask him, "Who are you?" They knew it was the Lord. Jesus came, took the bread, and gave it to them. He did the same with the fish. This was now the third time Jesus appeared to his disciples after he was raised from the dead.*

**John 21:1-14 (CEB)**

Always pay attention to the end of a book. In a mystery, it is where the loose ends are neatly tied up. In a biography, the end outlines the significance of a person's life, their legacy, if you will. In a history book, the final pages are usually an interpretation of the event(s). For poetry, it is the poem that the poet wanted to leave with the reader. The end of a book is important. This fishing tale is the last episode in the *Gospel of John*.

When you hear the lines from the end of John 20:30-31, "Then Jesus did many other miraculous signs in his disciples' presence, signs that aren't recorded in this scroll. But these things are written so that you will believe that Jesus is the Christ, God's Son, and that believing, you will have life in his name," it sounds like "The End." You expect the credits to begin rolling. The story is over.

And yet, there is more. It is almost as if *John* were saying, "I didn't get to tell you everything, but here is one more thing I can't leave out." Some commentators have seen this as an epilogue added later. Maybe it was even a different writer who heard this story and did not want it to be forgotten. However it came to be, we are lucky to have it.

The "epilogue" begins with "later." Obviously sometime after the Resurrection, after Jesus empowers the disciples by breathing the Spirit into them. Later.

Peter and others—six others to be exact—are hanging around. We don't know where or why. We don't know how much later. Simply "later," this group of seven was together. Peter announced, "I'm going fishing!" A statement like that in the twenty-first century means, "I'm taking the day off!" "I'm taking a break." "I'm getting away!"

That is not what Peter meant. What he said was, "I'm going back to work! I was a fisherman before this Jesus showed up. Now that he is gone, I guess I'll go back to doing what I always did." The others said, "We might as well join you."

They worked all night. Hard, back-breaking work. Casting the net out and dragging it back in. Casting the net out, dragging it back in. Casting the net out and dragging it back in. Over and over and over. Time after time. Out, in. Out, in. The monotonous repetition of hard labor, all to no avail.

Then in the East, the sight they had all been waiting for, a slight brightening of the night sky. The slow dawn of a new day. In the half-light, they saw a silhouette—a lone figure on the beach about one hundred yards off.

A voice called out, "Any luck?"

The exhausted monosyllabic reply was, "No."

The dark figure said, "Cast on the right side of the boat."

This is an interesting detail. Cast on the right side. He didn't say, "Try again." "Work harder." "You can do it!" Right-handed people standing with spread legs for balance would cast off the left side of the boat. The natural swing of a right-handed person would be to the left. Jesus told those fellows, "Quit doing it like you always have. Try something new."

Don't do things like you always have. What is the definition of "insanity"? Doing the same thing over and over again expecting a different result. Jesus told the disciples after his resurrection to do things differently, in new ways.

How do we live life as disciples after the Resurrection? How are we to be the church of the Living Lord after the Resurrection? In new ways! Quit doing it like we always have.

What is the old joke? "How many Methodists does it take to change a light bulb?"

"Change? We can't change that light bulb! My grandmother gave the church that light bulb!"

Or this one: "How many psychiatrists does it take to change a light bulb?" "One, but the light bulb must want to change."

*John* remembered that moment in the boat, including the words, "the right side of the boat."

As the men are struggling to pull in this amazing catch, the disciple whom Jesus loved best said, "It is the Lord!" Even in the semi-darkness, this disciple "saw" who was on the beach, knew who he really was.

Next is one of my favorite parts of the story. Peter got so excited, he put on his clothes (because the men had stripped down to work during the night.) Yes, Peter grabbed his clothes, pulled them on, and jumped into the water. I don't know about you, but that is not usually what I do before I jump into a lake. I usually go in the other direction. I get undressed.

The scripture says Peter got dressed "for he was naked." Lewis Grizzard always said, "Do you know the difference between being NAY-ked and nekkid? NAY-ked means you ain't got no clothes on, and nekkid means you ain't got clothes on and you're up to something!"

Peter was NAY-ked. It is a little reminiscent of Adam and Eve in the garden. They were nekkid, so they hid themselves. Peter was going to approach the Lord, so he covered up. But still, he jumped into the water.

Peter swims the hundred yards to shore. He steps onto the beach, dripping wet, to find Jesus cooking bread and fish over a charcoal fire. Bread and fish, the same menu as the feeding of the five thousand when all ate abundantly and had leftovers. Bread and fish.

Over a charcoal fire. Some English translations miss the subtlety here. The word John uses is that of a *charcoal fire* while others use the simple word for *fire.* This is another wonderful detail. A charcoal fire has a distinct scent, different from a wood fire. Interestingly enough, *John* mentions another charcoal fire (18:18). People, including Peter, stood around a charcoal fire in the courtyard when Jesus was being tried. Peter denied being one of Jesus' students while warming himself at a charcoal fire.

Peter walks up the beach on the dawn of this new day to the smell of his own betrayal but is fed bread by the bread of life. Good storytelling evokes the smell of betrayal and nourishment, grace and forgiveness.

This episode is filled with details! All come together

to paint a wonderful picture. The names of the disciples, the darkness, the hard labor that required the men to strip down, a charcoal fire, even the number of fish— one hundred fifty-three. (Much has been written in commentaries and studies about the meaning of 153. It could simply be *John* remembering an enormous catch of fish. ("You can't imagine it! I'll never forget! There were 153 fish!") Nevertheless, this particular story of *John's*, the last one, has many interesting details.

The one detail that annoys me is the missing detail. So many details, but the author omits the name of "the disciple whom Jesus loved." Of all the things to leave off!

One tradition suggests that it was *John* himself. Out of modesty, *John* did not include his name, not only here but throughout the entire gospel. The name "John" does not appear as the name of one of Jesus' disciples anywhere in *John*. However, some think the disciple whom Jesus loved was Lazarus (11:35-36). Others say it was Nicodemus. Others point to the man born blind. My point is, we do not know this disciple's name.

My own thought here is that *John* omitted the name on purpose. He is ending the larger story with this last episode which took place after the Resurrection. The character who recognizes Jesus as Lord is the unnamed disciple whom Jesus loved. Obviously, *John* knew the identity and name of this person, so we must assume he intentionally left the name off. He wanted to make sure you know the name of the disciple whom Jesus loved.

This is the last thread in the tapestry. This final

square of the patchwork quilt is set in the time after the Resurrection. The name of the disciple whom Jesus loves is YOU! You are the disciple whom Jesus loves. You live in the days after the Resurrection. You are sustained and fed by the Lord each morning of each new day.

*John* did know who the actual person was, but he chose to end his account of Jesus' story in an open-ended way that would include you. *John* wanted us to know the unending—now and future—story of the Living Lord who loves his disciples.

Blessings on YOU, the disciple whom Jesus loved.

# Resources

Barclay, William. *The Gospel of John, Volumes 1 & 2*. The Daily Bible Studies Series. The Westminster Press, 1956.

Bonino, Jose Miguez and Nestor Oscar Miguez. *That You May Have Life – Encounters with Jesus in the Gospel of John*. The Mission Education and Cultivation Program Division for the Women's Division. General Board of Global Ministries of the United Methodist Church, 1991.

Brown, Jeannine K. *The Gospels as Stories – A Narrative Approach to Matthew, Mark, Luke, and John*. Baker Academic, 2020.

Brown, Raymond E. *The Gospel According to John – A New Translation with Introduction and Commentary*. John I-XII and John XIII-XXI. Volumes 29 and 29a. Doubleday & Company, 1986.

Buechner, Frederick. *Whistling in the Dark – A Doubter's Dictionary*. Harper One, 1993.

Burnshaw, Stanley. Editor and Introduction by. *The Poem Itself*. Schocken Books, 1967.

Craddock, Fred B. *The Gospels*. Interpreting Biblical Texts Series. Abingdon, 1981.

Davis, Donald. *Telling Your Own Stories*. August House, 1993

David, Donald. *Writing as a Second Language*. August House Publishers, 2000.

Evans, Rachel Held. *Inspired – Slaying Giants, Walking on Water, and Loving the Bible Again.* Nelson Books, 2018.

Frost, Robert. *The Poetry of Robert Frost.* Edited by Edward Connery Lathem. Holt, Rinehart, and Winston, 1967.

Hamilton, Adam. *John – The Gospel of Light and Life.* Abingdon Press, 2015.

Jordan, Clarence. *The Cotton Patch Version of Matthew and John (First Eight Chapters*). Association Press-Follett Publishing Co., 1970.

Jordan, Clarence. *The Cotton Patch Version of Paul's Epistles.* Association Press – A Koinonia Publication, 1968.

Kysar, Robert D. *Invitation to John.* A Short-Term Disciple Bible Study. Abingdon Press, 2007.

Levine, Amy-Jill. *Entering the Passion of Jesus – A Beginner's Guide to Holy Week.* Abingdon Press, 2018.

Levine, Amy-Jill. *Witness at the Cross – A Beginner's Guide to Holy Friday.* Abingdon Press, 2021.

Lucado, Max. *The Gospel of John.* Life Lessons. Livingston Corporation Thomas Nelson, 2007.

Meacham, Jon. *The Hope of Glory – Reflections on the Last Words of Jesus from the Cross.* Convergent, 2020.

Marsh, John. *Saint John.* The Pelican New Testament Commentaries. Penguin Books, 1976.

Matson, Mark A. *John.* Interpretation Bible Studies. Westminster John Knox, 2002.

Maynard, Charles W. *A Storyteller Looks At The Parables.* Market Square Books, 2022.

Moltmann, Jurgen. *Passion for Life – A Messianic Lifestyle.* Fortress Press, 1978.

Peterson, Eugene H. *Answering God – The Psalms As Tools For Prayer.* Harper One, 1990.

Peterson, Eugene H. *A Long Obedience in the Same Direction.* Intervarsity Press, 2021.

Peterson, Eugene H. *Tell It Slant – A Conversation on the Language of Jesus in His Stories and Prayers.* William B. Eerdmans Publishing Company, 2008.

Phillips, J. B. *Ring of Truth – A Translator's Testimony.* Harold Shaw Publishers, 1967.

Price, Reynolds. *Three Gospels.* Scribners, 2011.

Sloyan, Gerard. *John. Interpretation: A Bible Commentary for Teaching and Preaching.* John Knox Press, 1988.

Smith, D. Moody. *John – Proclamation Commentaries.* Fortress Press, 1976.

Taylor, Barbara Brown. *Leaving Church – A Memoir of Faith.* Harper Collins Publishers, 2006.

Tozer, A.W. *And He Dwelt Among Us – Teaching from the Gospel of John.* Bethany House, 2009.

Trueblood, Elton. *The Incendiary Fellowship.* Harper & Row Publishers, 1967.

Willis, Garry. *What the Gospels Meant.* Viking, 2008.

Wright, N.T. *John for Everyone. Parts One and Two.* Westminster John Knox Press, 2004.

Wright, N.T. and Michael F. Bird. *The New Testament in Its World – An Introduction to the History, Literature, and Theology of the First Christians.* Zondervan Academic, 2019.

*The Interpreter's Bible. Volume IX. Luke and John.* Abingdon Press, 1995.

## Tidings of Comfort and Joy

New Stories of Advent and Christmas from Master Storyteller, Charles Maynard

**CHARLES W. MAYNARD**

marketsquarebooks.com

# A STORYTELLER LOOKS AT

## The Parables

### CHARLES W. MAYNARD

marketsquarebooks.com

Made in the USA
Columbia, SC
02 December 2022

Improvising being
In the face
Of adversity,
In the faces
Of adversaries.
No sense
Waving the fist
Of blame
In the direction
Of oncoming traffic.

This fault
Isn't theirs
By any means.

There needs to be
A particularly
Steady hand
During the storm –
The one to come,
The spiritual ones
That are here.
And I am patient –
Trying, anyways.
I mean, attempting
To be patient,
Not striving to be irritating.

Waiting here

Temporarily

Until the tempest

Subsides –

Before leaving

The bad weather

Behind before

I moved

In another

Direction.

When Enough Is Too Much

The dirt underneath
Fingernails doesn't
Bother me.

There may be soon
Good honest hard work
Clutched there.

A single day's labor
Trying to please the boss
And God.

(Sometimes the one has
Delusions of grandeur in
Mankind's mindset.)

Everybody has opinions
Offering up their suggestions,
Riding tides.

Nobody asks for them.
The floodgates (the lips)
Open – spilling.

There are no cries
For mercy – not obvious.
Maybe oblivious.

Words take away innocence
And guilty perceptions invited
Deep within.

Misguided words take away
Pleasures and give rise to
False conceptions.

Is this really our fatality? –
A bombardment of possessions
Unasked? Unmasked?

Misconstrued misconceptions.
Too much information all
At once.

And then to blurt out
"Oh, I'm so sorry"
Without meaning.

There's some dirt that
Doesn't bother me –
Free it!

But enough is enough –
The lines are drawn in
Immaculate misconceptions.

Even if this means
A very personalized
Solitary confinement.

As if the world understands
As if the world needs
The discernment.

And that does not mean
Only dying is involved –
Breathe relief.

Dying, yes, is very much
A part of the process –
Deep embracing.

No deep embarrassing.
Not here. Not now. Silence
The rumors.

And so is the living part,
Needing  whole-hearted  people
to Follow through.

Mistakes come along with growth
And forgiveness jointly comes, too.
Channel that!

Please do not extinguish
The shine of someone
Else's sun.

Let them shine for once,
Or maybe twice. And again.
....and again.

The lines are drawn now.
With bare hands in dirt. See?
Over here.

Dry Spell

Sometimes
The words
Don't come –
Sometimes
The words
Don't come
Out accurate.

This happens
Depending on
Expectations –
My own or the
People listening.

My voice
Becomes
Silent –
For fear
Of not saying
What is exact
At the
appropriate
Moment in time.

If this streak
Happens
At a much

Greater length,
The situation
Grows into
A locked room –
Walls becoming
Taller,
Locking
The doors
And windows,
And closing out
The outside world
By all means
Possible
Becomes
A necessity.

Dragging this out
More time and space
Provides social norms
To become
More irritable.

The cycle warrants
A downwards spiral.

Relearning
To reach out
Through

Reaching inward
To find strength
And to overcome
Trepidations.

Grasp
The concept
Or gasp
In defeat.
Better to clutch
Learning new
Possibilities
Before
Descending
Into an unforgiving
Death revealing
Clenched fists

And mangled teeth.

Like Thoughts Crowding My Mind

The cat starts
By weaving
Around my feet.
I ignore her,
Trying to silence
My thinking.

Thriving for
Attention,
The cat jumps upon
The table
In front of me,
Voicing her
Opinions
As if she
Dances
In my head.

She twists and turns
Before rolling over
Onto her back
To let me know
It is alright
To rub her belly,
An act of trust.

And soon enough
She's had her share
Of play time.
She jumps off
The table
And scurries away.

Planting herself
On the windowsill
On the other side
Of the room
In curious
Inclination.

Purring contentment.

And eventually
The cat will
Come back,
Interrupting
The silence
Of what is given
Of the night.

Inevitable

I watch the time
Listlessly and persistently
Moving in stride
From now to whenever.

Each second passing
Is like raindrops,
Except in perfect syncopation
In life's overflowing puddle.

Each breath digs
The already shallow grave
A little bit more
Superficially.

Nobody Knows

Nobody must know
Because the news
Is none of their business.

My relationship
With God is my own.
That is what makes
The event personal.

Who is anyone
To say how God
Speaks to me
Or how I
Talk back to God?

Back off, please
Because I am doing
Rather well.

Sometimes God
Intervenes
With someone
Who already
Understands.

There is no masquerade.

Sometimes those
Moments
Are the dog
Laying at my feet
And the cat
Sleeping on my lap.

Those moments
Become the beset
Times in my life.
And everyone else
Is on a need to know
Basis.

Life

God's not dead –
Maybe I'm not
In the proper
Place to hear
Any breathing.

Or just maybe
I have no
Way of knowing
How to get
A pulse.

For The Record

All the faces
Of the crow –
So many empty
And having
Conversations
That don't mean
Anything.

Someone held
Overnight
For observation –
    In the hospital
For being
Physically broken or
    In jail
For being
Heartbroken.

There are a lot
Of uncomfortable
Things happening
Which nobody
Speaks about,
As though it is
Taboo.

Every word,
Every action
Results in equal
And opposite
Words
And reactions.

(There are faces
Glazed over
With boredom!)

There are
No secrets here,
Just those
Who are
Less observant.

Everybody knows
Something
But not
Everybody wants
To understand
Or acknowledge.

All are in
One accord,
Or so it seems.

Time stands
Still –
A mended
Illusion.

Judgement day
Has come
And gone,
The future
Has been
Written
And so many
People
Are oblivious.

Subsist

Autumnal rains
Are normal –
Damp leaves
Covering
Muddy pathways
Taking me home.

The purpose
Of existing
Is questioned
Time and
Time and
Time again.

The future's fate
Is carried upon
The shoulders
Of now.

The fate
Of the world
Does not depend
On me –
Just the world
Of some
Around me.

We've reached
Our hands out
To pick each
Other up or
To see
Each other
Off in
A new
Direction.

To keep
The traffic
Moving
On life's highways –
Keeping the road rage
At bay.

Escape

We sit on the shore
Of Sam Dale Lake –
The park closed
At dusk, but
We're here anyways.

We don't fight
Others for
A proper position.

The fishing
May not be good,
But the conversation
Conveniently heads
In that direction.

Talking about
Younger days and
Younger ways.

The night guards us
With a passion
As stars stand watch,
The moon as their leader –
Heaven's astrological
Canopy.

The fish are sleeping
Under the lake
Of mirrored glass,
The fresh air
Valuable enough
To forget
The past shames
And fast claims.

Presence

What a waste
This is here
To merely
Take up
This space.

Stop staring –
There is nothing
To see here!

Move on!

Protection

I want to get in the vehicle,
And drive...
Travel around town
And onto the freeways.
Everything empty
Except the changing eyes
Of the traffic lights.

Finding comfort
In baron streets
And buildings that sleep –
Seeking wisdom
In the solemnness
And becoming lost
In the night's whispers.

What would be said
At every turn?

Instead I stand watch
From the front door,
Wondering about
The experience out there.
In its place, I attend
To the voices
On the home front

Wedding Announcement

Hey –
    We're
        getting
            married!

A Sling & A Stone

The oppositions
Of the past
Hide in the shadows

    Our alibis
     Eventually become
    Our lullabies

Check our selves
In the rearview
Mirrors, self-distraction.

Words will eventually
Dissolve like contrails
Without a glance.

Drive on through –
Wrap this around –
Running clear around.

Bored of rhetoric
Filling the surroundings –
Waiting to scream.

A restored life
Is unbiased –

A mere
Stone's throw away.

There's freedom from
The giants approaching
Within the shadows.

There's no need
For medical breakthroughs
Regarding these issues.

Just an awareness,
A spiritual awakening
To an understanding.

No lines forming,
Nobody asking "May
I assist you?"

This should be
A privileged opportunity,
Without moot points.

Jeremy

Sitting outside
On the tailgate
Of my pickup truck,
Summer night breezes
Kick up softly
Every now and then.
But we hardly notice.

He shares with me
His story, his past.
The portion of his existence
Continues to haunt him,
Sometimes keeping
Him up late at night –
Even after many years.

He questions if time
Really heals all wounds,
Or if the scars trigger
Digging up buried
Dilapidation.

He could have turned out
Differently than he has.

Maybe he should have

Turned out differently
Based on various statistics –
Based on skin color.
Based on age.
Based on family dynamics, Socio-
economic status,
Group memberships,
Political affiliations (or afflictions),
Elitism (or lack thereof),
Religious persuasion (or perversion)
Because data always shows
A greater chance of...

And he fulfilled a greater
Chance of that not occurring.

And in due time
He should have a moment –
    Of enlightenment,
    Of intervention
    Of freedom –
When God creates
A new world
For this young man.

Maybe next week
We will sit inside
The church instead

Of the church's parking lot
At 3 o'clock
In the morning.

Maybe next week
He will stand before
The church members
And proclaim
He's been released
Of the anger
And the frustration
And the terror
That's destroying him.

Maybe God will allow
Release of healing,
The walls broken down
Because of all the prayers
Provided for so long.

But this is about the people
Who have prayed.
It's about the young man
Sitting beside me
And his ability, eventually
To move on, to be released
And his opportunity
To stand like Peter

As a rock,
A cornerstone
For others
Who also scuffle
In the mental dynamics
Of good versus evil.

For tonight, though,
He has more time
To not cross over
That mountaintop.

Now is just
What he needs
To share his story.

Now is just.
Now is just.
Now is just...
Now is justified.

And I am
Attempting to wrap
My mind around
What has happened
To him.

For these precious moments,

The parking lot
Provides us the space
To understand where lines
Should have been drawn
Long ago.

Eventually, we'll be back
Inside.

Bitter

I don't like artificial flavors
This smile is a façade.

My spirit is in debt
That is overflowing
From deep within, like
A fountain turning
Into a waterfall turning
Into a swelling river
And muddy floodwaters.

There is sabotage in my life –
Admittance is the first step,
Isn't it? I'm tired of living
Unconsciously, having gone numb
And on the brink of death.

I'm tired of hiding
And the growing pains.
The hunger pangs commence –
Unnoticed at the beginning
Then the bitterness comes forth.

Tired of living in someone else's
Glossed over fabrications
That appear like truth.

I need Actual truth.

So whatever deceits

May fall by the wayside and get burned.

Room Without A View

The emptiness is overwhelming
God should be strong enough
To fill this void
Or am I too stubborn
To tear these walls down
To allow
God's appearance?

There is no knock on the door.
Then again, there is no door.
There is no point crying out
Since there is no way out (or in).
I'd take pride in workmanship
With the exception that I now
Stand alone.

There is no conclusion to this.
Not yet anyways. I don't know
If there are search parties seeking
Or if anyone realizes they should seek out.
This room, then, becomes a coffin.
A slow suffocation for a painless end. No!
Not yet.

There is a voice whispering faintly,
Almost muted from the rush hour of panic

And unnecessary thoughts clogging the mind.
"I have my reasons" for breath, for life.
"Just wait for Me" – and I start cracking
Under the pressure of unfamiliar fortitude
Rising. Intensifying.

Driven

Too many moments
Were left unguarded,
Merely vulnerable.

Is this instant
One of them?

My feet won't touch
The ground until
I arrive at
My destination.

Stopping only causes
Bewilderment.

This is not some
Repetitive drama –
      Same old stuff
        On a different day.
The scenery differentiates
Itself from yesterday
Because of the lighting,
The shadows.

We laugh at
Mediocrity, as if
Once an inside joke.

Independence has risen
Indeed,
To guide our path,
An open void
Far from lonely.

There are no debts
To society –
We owe nothing
And are owed
Nothing.

Taking refuge
On the open road –
Cadence of a
Freedom drive.

Friday Night Into Saturday Morning

The good night mantra
Needed spelling out
At times, but
Certainly not tonight.
These moments are both
Foreign and familiar.

No other intentions
But the one to have
And to hold this period –
Without holding back
For what the next phase
Brings.

There is nothing fantastic
To report on –
Nothing political,
No strangers interfering
With our lives in
Strange ways
And fear does not fit
Into the equation –
Not tonight, anyways.

This is unnatural –
Fitting comfortably
But artificial,
Awkward.

This is grace.
This is mercy.
This is the calm
From all the storms.
This is the song
Of a second chance –
Singing
      Without words
Playing
      Without music
Welcomed
      Without wrath.

To sleep is to miss
The pleasures
But to continue elicitation
Of relaxation
May bring new dreams To
a high state
Of mindful rest.

And this is making
All the difference.

Ghost Town

People standing in church
Or walking the boardwalk
Or shopping in crowded
    Barely lit streets
      Of a major city

The focus blends together –
An ad hoc museum
Of mannequins come to life,
Of sorts – in sorts.

Everyone is on a quest
Of happy-ness
Because we the people
Dreamed that freedom
To be "Me the individual"
And the self-indulgence
Leaves us invisible.

And we turn up empty.

Certain Age

There seems to come a time
When dreams and goals
Get lost in life's abyss.

There seems no chance
For all hope to live vicariously –
Common demise, gone away.

There seems to come an age
When, if we don't accomplish
Said goals and dreams and hopes,

Then there is little or no chance,
No anticipation, to achieve them
From that moment onward.

Trying and trying and trying.
The open door that is expected
Doesn't open, or the door becomes

The wrong way to traverse.
Without proper direction,
How can we know for sure?

There seems to come an age,
A line drawn that indicates
Turning around to assist others

Coming from behind us
And pushing them forward.
Someone flinches, closing doors.

There seems a time when
The line slows, or ceases to exist
And the other lines are too long.

How can we know for sure?
Once tricked into believing truth,
Becomes careful (or careless) action

Without the proper guidance.
Giving up may seem an option
When doing the day to day mundane.

When getting stuck within routine
Becomes so normal that reaching
Above and beyond is too much a stretch.

The body and the mind
Doesn't (or refuses) to extend
Or bend like in the youthful years.

To reach down to pick up
Where we once left off
Before ... before ...

There seems much soul searching
Is needed, but quickly halted
Because of the qualms of what

Would find even in the shallow end,
Let alone the deeper end of this pool –
The high dive scratched from the short list.

There is anxiety in beginning again
But maybe that isn't from the starting over
But having to go through the process –

The uncertainty of opening unlocked doors
That went unnoticed, or unchecked –
Or maybe just remained unknown.

There is the sense of rejection –
Or the someone mindlessly saying,
"You can't" or "You're no good."

Or those quotes being said
Inside the mind; the self-deprecating
Mentality falsely tilted as intuitive.

To not have time becomes the mantra
That spews forth from our mouths,
An excuse that should not be.

Attempting to backtrack
Is an enormous task
That becomes too overwhelming.

But living the current life track
Remains too underwhelming.
But giving up or giving in

Becomes the easiest tasks
To accomplish
    Or resuscitate.

Word Breath

I wait upon the morning sun
Flying in on a nightly squander.
I wait for you to speak, oh Lord,
And when you do, I'll ponder.

Cleansing

The storm lords itself
Over everyone equally.
The rains are unleashed
At an appointed time,
Catching some by surprise –
    Feet hit the ground
    Running for cover.
Not all are fond of moments
Such as these, but others
Find comfort in such a time.
The waters drenching –
This is the crowning glory,
With the exception
Of the lightning and thunder,
All the dirt swims away,
A natural springtime baptism.
Someone who wasn't ready
Shakes a clenched fist
And curses the skies (heavens).
The thunder claps, then rolls,
As if in response.
There's joy coming in the conclusion,
And ending when the clouds
Dissipate – Only to become a far-off
Memory someone may hold near
For dear life

No Doubt

God believes
In me
More than
I do
In Him.

Eventual

The night will soon
Be consumed
By the day.

If revelations
Like this
Point out
The obvious,
Then we are
Traveling
In the right direction.

3 A.M.

What is so fascinating
About the hour at hand?
The time comes around
At the same strike
Of the clock each day.

But I am here – awake – alone.
And eating a simple supper
On this brisk November
Friday morning – or maybe
This is Thursday night
(liable on who is asked) –
This is Friday,
Every time after midnight.

The time is early, careful.
Depending on a lot of criteria.
But here I am and maybe,
Just maybe, someone else
Is also awake in this moment.

And the time is spared
In sharing in pairs, or peace,
Or multiples there within,
Or thereof.

Oh – forget the technicalities.

Welcome to this moment –
No matter how asleep
Or awake you remain.

Equation

Tonight, I removed
All photographic
Evidence of you
From the albums,
Which are already
Collecting dust.

But the memories
Are more difficult
To delete –
Maybe forgetfulness
(With a pinch
Of forgiveness)
Will hinder those
Based on time
Plus distance
From every
Life event.

ACKNOWLEDGEMENTS

So many people have allowed me to succeed and fail throughout the process of the delivering of this book.

Special thanks to my parents, David and Laurel, for whom this book is dedicated. Also, a special thanks to Carrie and Allen, and their families. We've always taken the scenic route to get to every destination – and the journey to get here had its share of charming directions.

Special thanks to Stephen and Iko Blackmon, who were a guiding light in finding direction.

Honorary thanks to Ray and Helen - they loved us no matter what, supported us in our dreams, and were committed in being our biggest fans in the concerts of our lives.

Honorary thanks to Leonard and Ruth - for showing us what it means to live and to laugh and to love. Very grateful the desire for poetry passed down through the genes.

And the many thanks to family and friends through the adventures and inspirations.

**Author BIO**

Mark Maier is a poet with two new collections of poems, 13 8 and 3 A.M. Stories. These collected works are his first publications.

Mark grew up near Cleveland, Ohio. He graduated from Cleveland State University in 2000, where he was one of the student editors of their literary magazine.

After spending a couple years working in the newspaper industry in Ohio and Illinois, he found a niche working in the financial world as an accounting technician.

He holds a love for travel. He holds a fondness for attending poetry open mic nights – a mutual consideration of listening to poets impart their creations as well as revealing his works.

He currently lives in Columbus, Ohio with two cats.

**Stay Connected With Mark**

Go to https://dsmstoryforge.com/dsm-authors/mark-maier/ to get connected with Mark, follow him on social media, and see what else he is publishing and writing about these days!

Made in the USA
Columbia, SC
02 December 2022